50 Japan Restaurant Premium Food Recipes for Home

By: Kelly Johnson

Table of Contents

- Wagyu Beef Shabu-Shabu
- Sukiyaki
- Chirashi Sushi
- Omakase Sushi
- Tempura Udon
- Kaiseki Bento Box
- Kobe Beef Steak
- Miso Ramen
- Unagi Donburi
- Yakiniku
- Okonomiyaki
- Takoyaki
- Katsu Curry
- Yuba (Tofu Skin) Salad
- Tonkotsu Ramen
- Ebi Fry (Fried Shrimp)
- Soba Noodles with Dipping Sauce
- Nabe (Hot Pot)
- Hiyayakko (Cold Tofu)
- Ebi Chili
- Miso Glazed Black Cod
- Japanese Style Fried Rice
- Gyudon (Beef Bowl)
- Chicken Teriyaki
- Spicy Tuna Don
- Zaru Soba (Chilled Soba Noodles)
- Shabu-Shabu Salad
- Japanese Cheesecake
- Matcha Tiramisu
- Mochi Ice Cream
- Kakigori (Shaved Ice)
- Red Bean Soup (Zenzai)

- Japanese Pumpkin Tempura
- Yakitori (Grilled Chicken Skewers)
- Shirasu (Whitebait) Rice Bowl
- Mentaiko Pasta
- Takoyaki Okonomiyaki
- Sukiyaki Beef Rolls
- Goya Champuru (Bitter Melon Stir-Fry)
- Tempura Soba
- Katsu Sandwich
- Yakimeshi (Fried Rice)
- Miso Soup with Clams
- Kake Udon
- Korean BBQ Beef
- Shiro Ebi (White Shrimp) Tempura
- Saba Misoni (Miso Braised Mackerel)
- Nasu Dengaku (Miso Grilled Eggplant)
- Wasabi Mashed Potatoes
- Shiso and Almond Cookies

Wagyu Beef Shabu-Shabu

Ingredients:

- **For the Shabu-Shabu:**
    - 8 oz (225 g) Wagyu beef, thinly sliced (about 1/8-inch thick, preferably from the ribeye or sirloin)
    - 4 cups (960 ml) dashi broth (or beef broth)
    - 1 tablespoon soy sauce
    - 1 tablespoon mirin (sweet rice wine)
    - 1 teaspoon sake (optional)
    - 1 cup shiitake mushrooms, sliced
    - 1 cup Napa cabbage, chopped into bite-sized pieces
    - 1 cup enoki mushrooms, trimmed
    - 1 cup baby bok choy or spinach
    - 1 cup tofu, cut into cubes
    - 1-2 green onions, sliced (for garnish)
    - 1 tablespoon sesame seeds (for garnish)
- **For the Dipping Sauces:**
    - **Ponzu Sauce:**
        - 1/4 cup (60 ml) soy sauce
        - 1/4 cup (60 ml) yuzu juice (or lemon juice)
        - 1 tablespoon rice vinegar
        - 1 teaspoon sugar
    - **Goma (Sesame) Sauce:**
        - 1/4 cup (60 ml) tahini or sesame paste
        - 2 tablespoons soy sauce
        - 2 tablespoons mirin
        - 1 tablespoon sugar
        - 1 tablespoon rice vinegar
        - 1 tablespoon water (to thin, if needed)

Instructions:

1. **Prepare the Broth:**
    - In a large pot, combine the dashi broth, soy sauce, mirin, and sake (if using). Bring to a gentle simmer over medium heat. Adjust the seasoning to taste.
2. **Prepare the Vegetables and Tofu:**
    - While the broth is heating, prepare the vegetables and tofu. Arrange them on a serving platter or individual plates for easy access at the table.
3. **Prepare the Dipping Sauces:**
    - For the ponzu sauce, combine soy sauce, yuzu juice (or lemon juice), rice vinegar, and sugar in a small bowl. Stir until the sugar is dissolved.

- For the goma (sesame) sauce, whisk together tahini or sesame paste, soy sauce, mirin, sugar, rice vinegar, and water in another bowl until smooth. Adjust the consistency with additional water if needed.

4. **Cook the Shabu-Shabu:**
   - Once the broth is simmering, transfer the pot to the table, where it can continue to simmer gently. Use chopsticks or a slotted spoon to cook the ingredients.
   - Add a few slices of Wagyu beef to the broth at a time, allowing them to cook for about 10-20 seconds, or until they change color and are cooked through. Remove the beef with chopsticks or a slotted spoon and dip into the dipping sauces.
   - Add vegetables and tofu to the pot and cook until tender. The cooking time for vegetables will vary depending on the type.

5. **Serve:**
   - Arrange the cooked Wagyu beef, vegetables, and tofu on individual plates.
   - Serve with dipping sauces on the side.
   - Garnish with sliced green onions and sesame seeds if desired.

Notes:

- **Wagyu Beef:** For the best results, use high-quality Wagyu beef with a good amount of marbling. The thin slices will cook quickly in the hot broth.
- **Broth:** You can use store-bought dashi broth or make your own by simmering kombu (seaweed) and bonito flakes in water. Alternatively, beef broth can be used.
- **Dipping Sauces:** Both ponzu and goma sauces complement the rich flavor of Wagyu beef. Adjust the ingredients to your taste preferences.
- **Vegetables and Tofu:** Feel free to add other vegetables such as carrots, radishes, or mushrooms based on your preference.

Wagyu Beef Shabu-Shabu is a delightful and interactive dining experience, where you get to cook and enjoy each ingredient at the table. It's perfect for a cozy meal with family or friends. Enjoy!

Sukiyaki

Ingredients:

- **For the Sukiyaki:**
    - 8 oz (225 g) thinly sliced beef (such as sirloin or ribeye)
    - 1 tablespoon vegetable oil
    - 1 cup shiitake mushrooms, sliced
    - 1 cup Napa cabbage, chopped into bite-sized pieces
    - 1 cup sliced onions
    - 1 cup tofu, cut into cubes
    - 1 cup shirataki noodles (konjac noodles), rinsed and drained (or use udon noodles)
    - 1 cup sliced scallions
    - 1/2 cup sugar
    - 1/4 cup soy sauce
    - 1/4 cup mirin (sweet rice wine)
    - 1/4 cup sake (optional)
    - 1/2 cup dashi broth (or water)
- **For Serving:**
    - Cooked rice
    - Raw eggs (optional, for dipping)

Instructions:

1. **Prepare the Ingredients:**
    - Slice the beef into thin strips if not pre-sliced.
    - Prepare all vegetables, tofu, and noodles as described. Arrange them on a large platter for easy access.
2. **Prepare the Sauce (Sukiyaki Sauce):**
    - In a bowl, mix together the sugar, soy sauce, mirin, sake (if using), and dashi broth. Stir until the sugar is dissolved and set aside.
3. **Cook the Sukiyaki:**
    - Heat vegetable oil in a large, deep skillet or a sukiyaki pot over medium heat.
    - Add the beef to the pot and cook until it starts to brown.
    - Add the shiitake mushrooms, onions, and any other vegetables that need longer cooking times. Stir and cook for a few minutes.
    - Pour the sukiyaki sauce over the beef and vegetables. Stir well to combine and allow it to simmer gently.
4. **Add Remaining Ingredients:**
    - Add the tofu and shirataki noodles (or udon noodles) to the pot. Stir gently and let them cook until heated through.
    - Continue to simmer until all ingredients are cooked to your desired tenderness.

5. **Serve:**
   - Serve the Sukiyaki directly from the pot or skillet to individual bowls. Each person can dip their ingredients into a raw egg (if using) for added richness, or simply enjoy as is.
   - Accompany with bowls of cooked rice on the side.

Notes:

- **Beef:** Use high-quality beef with good marbling for the best flavor. Thinly sliced beef is key for quick cooking and tender texture.
- **Vegetables and Tofu:** Sukiyaki is highly customizable. Feel free to add other vegetables like mushrooms, carrots, or daikon radish according to your preference.
- **Shirataki Noodles:** These are traditional in Sukiyaki, but you can substitute with udon noodles or rice noodles if desired.
- **Raw Egg:** The raw egg is a traditional accompaniment and adds a rich flavor. However, you can omit it if you prefer not to use raw egg.
- **Dashi Broth:** For an authentic flavor, use dashi broth. If unavailable, water can be used as a substitute, though it will be less flavorful.

Sukiyaki is a delightful dish that combines savory and sweet flavors with a communal cooking experience. It's perfect for a cozy meal with family or friends. Enjoy!

Chirashi Sushi

Ingredients:

- **For the Sushi Rice:**
    - 2 cups sushi rice
    - 2 1/2 cups water
    - 1/4 cup rice vinegar
    - 3 tablespoons sugar
    - 1 tablespoon salt
- **For the Toppings:**
    - 6 oz (170 g) sashimi-grade tuna, sliced
    - 6 oz (170 g) sashimi-grade salmon, sliced
    - 1/2 cup cucumber, julienned
    - 1/2 cup daikon radish, julienned
    - 1/2 cup carrots, julienned
    - 1/2 avocado, sliced
    - 1/4 cup pickled ginger
    - 2-3 sheets nori (seaweed), cut into strips
    - 1 tablespoon sesame seeds
    - 2 tablespoons soy sauce (for serving)
    - 2 tablespoons wasabi (for serving)
- **Optional Garnishes:**
    - Sliced green onions
    - Shredded or sliced omelet (tamago)
    - Edamame
    - Shiso leaves

Instructions:

1. **Prepare the Sushi Rice:**
    - Rinse the sushi rice under cold water until the water runs clear to remove excess starch.
    - In a rice cooker, combine the rinsed rice and water. Cook according to the manufacturer's instructions.
    - While the rice is cooking, prepare the sushi vinegar mixture. In a small saucepan, heat rice vinegar, sugar, and salt over low heat, stirring until the sugar and salt are completely dissolved. Allow to cool.
    - Once the rice is cooked, transfer it to a large bowl. Gently fold in the sushi vinegar mixture with a wooden spatula or rice paddle. Allow the rice to cool to room temperature.
2. **Prepare the Toppings:**
    - Slice the sashimi-grade tuna and salmon into thin pieces.

- Julienne the cucumber, daikon radish, and carrots. Slice the avocado.
- Cut the nori sheets into thin strips.
- Prepare any additional garnishes if using.
3. **Assemble the Chirashi Sushi:**
    - Spoon a portion of the sushi rice into individual serving bowls or a large serving dish.
    - Arrange the sashimi, cucumber, daikon radish, carrots, and avocado artfully over the rice.
    - Garnish with pickled ginger, nori strips, sesame seeds, and optional garnishes such as green onions or omelet slices.
4. **Serve:**
    - Serve the Chirashi Sushi with soy sauce and wasabi on the side.
    - Each person can add soy sauce and wasabi to taste.

Notes:

- **Sushi Rice:** Properly seasoning and cooling the sushi rice is crucial for the right texture and flavor. Allow the rice to cool to room temperature before adding toppings.
- **Toppings:** Chirashi Sushi is highly customizable. Feel free to add other ingredients such as cooked shrimp, eel, or pickled vegetables.
- **Sashimi:** Use high-quality, fresh sashimi-grade fish for the best results. If you prefer not to use raw fish, you can substitute with cooked seafood or additional vegetables.
- **Nori:** Cut the nori into strips just before serving to maintain its crispness.

Chirashi Sushi is a colorful and delicious dish that brings a touch of elegance to any meal. It's perfect for showcasing seasonal ingredients and enjoying a variety of flavors in one bowl.

Omakase Sushi

Ingredients:

- **For Sushi Rice:**
    - 2 cups sushi rice
    - 2 1/2 cups water
    - 1/4 cup rice vinegar
    - 3 tablespoons sugar
    - 1 tablespoon salt
- **For Sushi Toppings:**
    - 6 oz (170 g) sashimi-grade tuna, thinly sliced
    - 6 oz (170 g) sashimi-grade salmon, thinly sliced
    - 6 oz (170 g) yellowtail, thinly sliced
    - 4 oz (115 g) cooked shrimp, peeled and deveined
    - 4 oz (115 g) eel (unagi), grilled and sliced
    - 1 avocado, sliced
    - 1 cucumber, julienned
    - 1 small daikon radish, julienned
    - 1/4 cup pickled ginger
    - 2-3 sheets nori (seaweed), cut into strips
    - Soy sauce (for dipping)
    - Wasabi (for serving)
    - Pickled wasabi stem or fresh wasabi (optional)
    - Microgreens or edible flowers (for garnish)

Instructions:

1. **Prepare the Sushi Rice:**
    - Rinse the sushi rice under cold water until the water runs clear to remove excess starch.
    - Cook the rice in a rice cooker or according to the package instructions.
    - While the rice is cooking, mix the rice vinegar, sugar, and salt in a small saucepan over low heat until the sugar and salt dissolve. Allow to cool.
    - Once the rice is cooked, transfer it to a large bowl. Gently fold in the vinegar mixture with a wooden spatula or rice paddle. Allow to cool to room temperature.
2. **Prepare the Sushi Toppings:**
    - Slice sashimi-grade fish into thin slices.
    - Prepare additional ingredients such as cooked shrimp, eel, avocado, cucumber, and daikon radish.
    - Slice nori into thin strips if using.
3. **Assemble the Omakase Sushi:**

- **Nigiri Sushi:** Shape small balls of sushi rice and press a slice of sashimi or other toppings on top.
- **Sashimi:** Arrange slices of sashimi-grade fish on a platter.
- **Maki Rolls:** Prepare simple rolls with nori, sushi rice, and fillings like avocado, cucumber, or fish (optional).
- **Temaki (Hand Rolls):** Fill nori sheets with sushi rice, fish, and vegetables, and roll into cones.

4. **Serve:**
   - Arrange the sushi on a large platter or individual plates.
   - Serve with soy sauce, pickled ginger, and wasabi on the side.
   - Garnish with microgreens or edible flowers for a decorative touch.

Notes:

- **Freshness:** The key to an excellent omakase sushi experience is the freshness of the ingredients. Use high-quality, sashimi-grade fish and other fresh components.
- **Variety:** An omakase meal often includes a variety of sushi types, so include a mix of nigiri, sashimi, and rolls to create a well-rounded experience.
- **Presentation:** Presentation is crucial in an omakase setting. Arrange the sushi beautifully and consider adding garnishes to enhance the visual appeal.
- **Customizing:** Feel free to customize the ingredients based on your preferences or what's available. You might include unique items like toro (fatty tuna), uni (sea urchin), or seasonal vegetables.

Omakase Sushi is about trust and experience. By selecting the best ingredients and presenting them thoughtfully, you can create an enjoyable and memorable sushi experience similar to dining at a top sushi restaurant. Enjoy your culinary adventure!

Tempura Udon

Ingredients:

- **For the Udon Soup:**
    - 4 cups dashi broth (or water with a dashi packet)
    - 1/4 cup soy sauce
    - 2 tablespoons mirin (sweet rice wine)
    - 1 tablespoon sake (optional)
    - 2-3 green onions, sliced
    - 1 cup sliced mushrooms (shiitake, enoki, or your choice)
    - 1 cup baby bok choy or spinach
    - 2 servings fresh udon noodles (or dried udon noodles, cooked according to package instructions)
- **For the Tempura:**
    - 1 cup all-purpose flour
    - 1/2 cup cornstarch
    - 1 teaspoon baking powder
    - 1 cup cold sparkling water (or ice-cold water)
    - Vegetable oil for frying
    - 1 large sweet potato, sliced thinly
    - 1 small zucchini, sliced thinly
    - 1 cup shrimp, peeled and deveined
- **Optional Garnishes:**
    - 1 tablespoon toasted sesame seeds
    - Pickled ginger
    - Nori (seaweed) strips

Instructions:

1. **Prepare the Tempura:**
    - **Make the Tempura Batter:** In a bowl, combine flour, cornstarch, and baking powder. Gradually add cold sparkling water and mix lightly until just combined. The batter should be lumpy; do not overmix.
    - **Heat the Oil:** In a deep pot or fryer, heat vegetable oil to 350°F (175°C). Use enough oil to submerge the tempura pieces.
    - **Fry the Tempura:** Dip the sweet potato, zucchini, and shrimp into the batter and carefully place them into the hot oil. Fry in batches to avoid overcrowding. Cook until golden and crispy, about 2-3 minutes for vegetables and 1-2 minutes for shrimp. Remove with a slotted spoon and drain on paper towels.
2. **Prepare the Udon Soup:**
    - **Make the Broth:** In a pot, combine dashi broth, soy sauce, mirin, and sake (if using). Bring to a simmer over medium heat.

- **Add Vegetables:** Add sliced mushrooms and cook until tender, about 3-4 minutes. Add baby bok choy or spinach and cook for an additional 1-2 minutes.
- **Cook Udon Noodles:** If using dried udon noodles, cook according to the package instructions. If using fresh noodles, briefly blanch them in boiling water until heated through. Drain and set aside.
3. **Assemble the Dish:**
    - **Combine Noodles and Broth:** Divide the cooked udon noodles into serving bowls. Ladle the hot broth with vegetables over the noodles.
    - **Top with Tempura:** Place the tempura pieces on top of the noodles and broth.
4. **Garnish and Serve:**
    - **Garnish:** Sprinkle with sliced green onions, toasted sesame seeds, and optional garnishes like pickled ginger or nori strips.
    - **Serve:** Serve hot and enjoy!

Notes:

- **Dashi Broth:** Traditional dashi broth gives the soup a deep umami flavor. You can use instant dashi powder if making fresh dashi isn't feasible.
- **Tempura Batter:** The key to crispy tempura is a cold batter and hot oil. Ensure the oil temperature remains consistent while frying.
- **Udon Noodles:** Fresh udon noodles are ideal, but dried noodles are a good alternative. Be sure to cook them properly and rinse them if needed.
- **Customizing:** Feel free to add other vegetables or proteins to the tempura, such as bell peppers, mushrooms, or tofu.

Tempura Udon is a delicious and satisfying dish that combines the savory flavors of the broth with the light, crispy texture of tempura. It's perfect for a comforting meal any time of the year. Enjoy!

Kaiseki Bento Box

Components:

1. **Rice and Main Protein**
2. **Vegetable and Side Dishes**
3. **Pickles and Condiments**
4. **Soup or Broth (optional)**
5. **Dessert**

Ingredients:

For the Rice:

- 1 cup sushi rice
- 1 1/4 cups water
- 2 tablespoons rice vinegar
- 1 tablespoon sugar
- 1/2 teaspoon salt

For the Main Protein:

- **Grilled Salmon:**
    - 2 salmon fillets
    - Salt and pepper
    - Lemon wedges (for garnish)
    - Soy sauce (optional)

For the Vegetable and Side Dishes:

- **Simmered Vegetables:**
    - 1 small carrot, sliced
    - 1 small daikon radish, sliced
    - 1 cup baby potatoes, halved
    - 1 tablespoon soy sauce
    - 1 tablespoon mirin
    - 1 cup dashi broth (or water)
- **Braised Tofu:**
    - 1 block firm tofu, cut into cubes
    - 2 tablespoons soy sauce
    - 1 tablespoon mirin
    - 1/2 cup dashi broth (or water)
    - 1 teaspoon sesame oil

For the Pickles and Condiments:

- **Japanese Pickles (Tsukemono):**
    - Store-bought or homemade pickled vegetables, such as pickled daikon radish, cucumber, or cabbage.

For the Soup (optional):

- **Miso Soup:**
    - 2 cups dashi broth
    - 2 tablespoons miso paste
    - 1/2 cup tofu, cubed
    - 1/4 cup sliced green onions
    - Seaweed strips (optional)

For the Dessert:

- **Fruit or Sweet Treats:**
    - Fresh fruit (e.g., sliced apple, orange segments)
    - Traditional Japanese sweets (e.g., mochi, dorayaki)

Instructions:

1. **Prepare the Rice:**
    - Rinse the sushi rice under cold water until the water runs clear.
    - Cook the rice in a rice cooker or pot according to the package instructions.
    - Once cooked, transfer the rice to a bowl and gently fold in rice vinegar, sugar, and salt. Allow to cool.
2. **Prepare the Main Protein:**
    - **Grilled Salmon:** Season the salmon fillets with salt and pepper. Grill or pan-sear until cooked through, about 4-5 minutes per side. Garnish with lemon wedges and a drizzle of soy sauce if desired.
3. **Prepare the Vegetable and Side Dishes:**
    - **Simmered Vegetables:** In a pot, combine carrots, daikon, baby potatoes, soy sauce, mirin, and dashi broth. Simmer until the vegetables are tender, about 15-20 minutes. Drain and cool.
    - **Braised Tofu:** In a skillet, heat sesame oil and add tofu cubes. Cook until lightly browned. Add soy sauce, mirin, and dashi broth. Simmer until the tofu absorbs the flavors, about 10 minutes. Cool.
4. **Prepare the Pickles and Condiments:**
    - Arrange a selection of Japanese pickles in small compartments of the bento box.
5. **Prepare the Soup (Optional):**
    - In a pot, heat dashi broth and dissolve miso paste in it. Add tofu cubes and heat gently. Garnish with green onions and seaweed strips if desired.
6. **Prepare the Dessert:**

- Arrange fresh fruit or traditional Japanese sweets in a separate section of the bento box.
7. **Assemble the Bento Box:**
   - Place a portion of sushi rice in one compartment.
   - Arrange the grilled salmon, simmered vegetables, and braised tofu in separate compartments.
   - Add pickles and condiments.
   - Include the soup in a small container if desired.
   - Finish with a section for fruit or sweets.

Notes:

- **Presentation:** A kaiseki bento box should be beautifully arranged, with a focus on seasonal ingredients and balanced flavors. Use small, compartmentalized containers or sections of the bento box to showcase each item.
- **Customizing:** Feel free to adjust the ingredients based on personal preference or seasonal availability. The variety and balance of flavors are key to a successful kaiseki bento.
- **Storage:** If preparing in advance, keep the components refrigerated and assemble the box just before serving to ensure freshness.

Kaiseki Bento Box is a delightful and elegant way to enjoy a variety of Japanese flavors in one meal. It combines the artistry of kaiseki with the convenience of a bento, making it perfect for special occasions or a refined everyday meal. Enjoy!

Kobe Beef Steak

Ingredients:

- **For the Kobe Beef Steak:**
    - 2 Kobe beef steaks (about 6-8 oz each)
    - Salt (preferably sea salt or kosher salt)
    - Freshly ground black pepper
    - 1 tablespoon vegetable oil or clarified butter (for searing)
    - 2 cloves garlic, crushed (optional)
    - 1 sprig rosemary or thyme (optional)
- **For the Garnish (Optional):**
    - Sea salt flakes
    - Fresh herbs (e.g., parsley, chives)
    - Lemon wedges

Instructions:

1. **Prepare the Steak:**
    - **Bring to Room Temperature:** Remove the Kobe beef steaks from the refrigerator and let them come to room temperature for about 30 minutes before cooking. This ensures even cooking.
2. **Season the Steak:**
    - **Season Generously:** Pat the steaks dry with paper towels. Season both sides with salt and freshly ground black pepper. Be generous with the seasoning, as this will enhance the flavor of the beef.
3. **Heat the Pan:**
    - **Preheat the Pan:** Heat a heavy skillet or cast-iron pan over medium-high heat until very hot. You can also use a grill if preferred.
    - **Add Oil:** Add vegetable oil or clarified butter to the pan and swirl to coat. The oil should shimmer but not smoke excessively.
4. **Cook the Steak:**
    - **Sear the Steak:** Place the steaks in the hot pan and cook without moving them for about 2-3 minutes on each side, or until a rich, brown crust forms. For medium-rare doneness, aim for an internal temperature of 130-135°F (54-57°C). Adjust the cooking time based on your preferred level of doneness.
    - **Add Aromatics (Optional):** If desired, add crushed garlic and a sprig of rosemary or thyme to the pan during the last minute of cooking for added flavor. Baste the steaks with the aromatic-infused oil using a spoon.
5. **Rest the Steak:**
    - **Let Rest:** Transfer the cooked steaks to a plate and cover loosely with foil. Let them rest for 5-10 minutes. Resting allows the juices to redistribute, ensuring a tender and juicy steak.

6. **Serve:**
    - **Garnish and Serve:** Slice the steak if desired, or serve whole. Garnish with sea salt flakes and fresh herbs. Serve with lemon wedges on the side for a touch of brightness.

Notes:

- **Cooking Doneness:** Kobe beef is best enjoyed medium-rare to rare due to its tenderness and high fat content. Adjust cooking times based on your preferred doneness, but be careful not to overcook, as it can diminish the quality of the meat.
- **Pan Choice:** A heavy skillet or cast-iron pan is ideal for achieving a good sear. If using a grill, preheat it well and ensure it's hot before placing the steaks on it.
- **Pairings:** Kobe beef pairs beautifully with simple sides such as sautéed vegetables, mashed potatoes, or a fresh salad. The focus should be on the steak itself, given its premium quality.
- **Storage:** If you have leftovers, store them in an airtight container in the refrigerator. Reheat gently to avoid overcooking.

Kobe Beef Steak is a luxurious treat that celebrates the rich flavors and tender texture of one of the world's most renowned types of beef. Whether served as a special occasion meal or a refined everyday treat, this steak promises an exceptional dining experience. Enjoy!

Miso Ramen

Ingredients:

For the Broth:

- 4 cups chicken or vegetable broth
- 2 cups water
- 1/4 cup white miso paste
- 2 tablespoons red miso paste (for added depth)
- 1 tablespoon soy sauce
- 1 tablespoon sake (optional)
- 1 tablespoon mirin (sweet rice wine)
- 2 cloves garlic, minced
- 1-inch piece of ginger, grated

For the Toppings:

- 2 servings fresh or dried ramen noodles
- 1 cup sliced mushrooms (shiitake, button, or your choice)
- 1 cup baby spinach or bok choy
- 1 cup cooked chicken, pork, or tofu (sliced or shredded)
- 2 soft-boiled eggs (marinated or plain)
- 1/4 cup corn kernels (optional)
- 2-3 green onions, sliced
- 1/4 cup sliced bamboo shoots (optional)
- 1 sheet nori (seaweed), cut into strips (optional)
- Sesame seeds for garnish
- Bean sprouts (optional)

For the Marinade (Optional for Eggs):

- 1/4 cup soy sauce
- 1/4 cup mirin
- 1/4 cup water
- 1 tablespoon sugar

Instructions:

1. **Prepare the Broth:**
    - **Combine Ingredients:** In a large pot, combine chicken or vegetable broth with water. Bring to a simmer over medium heat.

- **Add Miso Paste:** Stir in white and red miso paste, soy sauce, sake, and mirin. Whisk until miso paste is fully dissolved. Add minced garlic and grated ginger. Simmer for 10-15 minutes, allowing flavors to meld. Adjust seasoning to taste.

2. **Prepare the Toppings:**
    - **Cook the Noodles:** Cook ramen noodles according to the package instructions. Drain and set aside.
    - **Prepare the Vegetables:** In a separate pan, sauté mushrooms until tender. Blanch baby spinach or bok choy in boiling water for 1-2 minutes, then drain and set aside.
    - **Prepare the Protein:** Cook or reheat your choice of protein (chicken, pork, or tofu). Slice or shred as needed.
    - **Marinate the Eggs (Optional):** For marinated eggs, combine soy sauce, mirin, water, and sugar in a bowl. Marinate soft-boiled eggs in this mixture for 1-2 hours, then peel.

3. **Assemble the Ramen:**
    - **Divide Noodles:** Place cooked ramen noodles into serving bowls.
    - **Add Broth:** Ladle hot miso broth over the noodles.
    - **Top with Ingredients:** Arrange sliced mushrooms, cooked protein, baby spinach or bok choy, corn, bamboo shoots, and marinated or plain eggs on top of the noodles.
    - **Garnish:** Add sliced green onions, nori strips, sesame seeds, and bean sprouts if desired.

4. **Serve:**
    - Serve the miso ramen hot. Enjoy with chopsticks and a soup spoon.

Notes:

- **Miso Paste:** You can use different types of miso paste based on your preference. White miso is milder and sweeter, while red miso is stronger and saltier. Mixing both gives a balanced flavor.
- **Broth Base:** For a richer broth, you can use a combination of chicken stock and dashi. You can also add a dash of white wine or a bit of soy sauce to enhance the depth of flavor.
- **Toppings:** Customize your ramen with various toppings according to your taste. Common additions include bamboo shoots, corn, mushrooms, and marinated eggs.
- **Make Ahead:** The broth can be made in advance and stored in the refrigerator for up to 3 days. Reheat before serving.

Miso Ramen is a versatile and comforting dish perfect for any time of the year. It brings together the umami richness of miso with the satisfying textures of ramen noodles and fresh toppings. Enjoy creating this flavorful bowl of ramen at home!

Unagi Donburi

Ingredients:

For the Unagi (Grilled Eel):

- 2 unagi fillets (grilled eel, can be purchased pre-cooked from Asian grocery stores or online)
- 1/4 cup soy sauce
- 1/4 cup mirin (sweet rice wine)
- 2 tablespoons sugar
- 2 tablespoons sake (optional)

For the Rice:

- 2 cups short-grain or sushi rice
- 2 1/2 cups water
- 2 tablespoons rice vinegar
- 1 tablespoon sugar
- 1/2 teaspoon salt

For Garnish:

- 1-2 green onions, thinly sliced
- Shredded nori (seaweed) or toasted sesame seeds
- Pickled ginger (optional)
- Shiso leaves or parsley (optional)

Instructions:

1. **Prepare the Rice:**
   - **Rinse the Rice:** Rinse the rice under cold water until the water runs clear to remove excess starch.
   - **Cook the Rice:** Combine rinsed rice and water in a rice cooker or pot. Cook according to the rice cooker instructions or simmer on the stovetop until water is absorbed and rice is tender, about 15-20 minutes.
   - **Season the Rice:** Once cooked, transfer rice to a bowl and gently fold in rice vinegar, sugar, and salt. Allow to cool slightly.
2. **Prepare the Unagi Sauce:**
   - **Make the Sauce:** In a small saucepan, combine soy sauce, mirin, sugar, and sake (if using). Bring to a simmer over medium heat and cook until the sauce slightly thickens, about 5 minutes. Remove from heat and let it cool.
3. **Prepare the Unagi (Grilled Eel):**

- **Grill or Heat the Eel:** If using pre-cooked eel, it typically comes with a separate packet of sauce. Heat the eel according to package instructions or grill it briefly to warm it up and enhance the flavor. Brush with some of the prepared sauce during grilling or heating.
- **Slice the Eel:** Cut the eel into bite-sized pieces or strips.

4. **Assemble the Unagi Donburi:**
   - **Serve the Rice:** Divide the seasoned rice among serving bowls.
   - **Top with Unagi:** Arrange slices of unagi over the rice.
   - **Add Sauce:** Drizzle the remaining sauce over the eel and rice.

5. **Garnish and Serve:**
   - **Add Garnishes:** Sprinkle with sliced green onions, shredded nori, and toasted sesame seeds. Add pickled ginger and fresh herbs if desired.
   - **Serve:** Enjoy hot!

Notes:

- **Eel Preparation:** Freshly grilled unagi is ideal, but if you're using pre-cooked eel, make sure it's thoroughly heated and coated with the sauce for best results.
- **Rice Choice:** Short-grain or sushi rice is preferred for its sticky texture, which helps hold the rice together and complements the eel.
- **Sauce:** Adjust the sweetness and saltiness of the sauce to your preference. You can also add a bit of mirin for additional sweetness or a splash of sake for depth.
- **Customization:** Feel free to add other toppings or sides like steamed vegetables or pickled vegetables to make the meal more substantial.

Unagi Donburi is a rich and flavorful dish that brings together the savory taste of grilled eel with the comforting texture of rice. It's a classic Japanese comfort food that's perfect for any occasion. Enjoy preparing and savoring this delicious meal!

Yakiniku

Ingredients:

For the Meat:

- 1 lb (450 g) beef ribeye, sirloin, or chuck, thinly sliced (alternatively, use pork or chicken)
- Salt and pepper, to taste

For the Marinade (Optional, for pre-marinated meat):

- 1/4 cup soy sauce
- 2 tablespoons mirin (sweet rice wine)
- 2 tablespoons sake (optional)
- 1 tablespoon sugar
- 1 tablespoon sesame oil
- 2 cloves garlic, minced
- 1-inch piece of ginger, minced

For the Yakiniku Sauce (Dip and Drizzle):

- 1/4 cup soy sauce
- 2 tablespoons mirin
- 2 tablespoons sake
- 1 tablespoon sugar
- 1 tablespoon sesame oil
- 1 clove garlic, minced
- 1 tablespoon grated ginger
- 1 tablespoon toasted sesame seeds (optional)
- 1-2 teaspoons gochujang (Korean red chili paste) or chili flakes (optional for spice)

For Accompaniments:

- Steamed white rice
- Sliced vegetables (e.g., bell peppers, onions, mushrooms, zucchini)
- Pickled vegetables (e.g., pickled daikon, cucumber)
- Fresh lettuce or shiso leaves (for wrapping)
- Sliced green onions
- Sesame seeds
- Additional dipping sauces or condiments (e.g., ponzu sauce, wasabi)

Instructions:

1. **Prepare the Meat:**

- **Slice the Meat:** Thinly slice the beef against the grain into bite-sized pieces. If using other meats, slice them accordingly.
- **Marinate (Optional):** If you want to marinate the meat, mix all marinade ingredients in a bowl. Add the meat slices and let them marinate in the refrigerator for at least 30 minutes, or up to 2 hours for more flavor.

2. **Prepare the Yakiniku Sauce:**
   - **Mix Ingredients:** In a small bowl, combine all the yakiniku sauce ingredients. Adjust sweetness or spiciness according to taste. Set aside.
3. **Cook the Meat:**
   - **Preheat the Grill or Pan:** If using a grill, preheat it to high heat. If using a grill pan or cast-iron skillet, heat it over medium-high heat until very hot.
   - **Grill the Meat:** Season the meat slices with salt and pepper. Grill or pan-cook the meat for about 1-2 minutes per side, or until cooked to your desired doneness. Do not overcrowd the grill or pan; cook in batches if necessary.
   - **Cook Vegetables:** If using vegetables, grill or sauté them alongside the meat, or separately, until tender and slightly charred.
4. **Serve:**
   - **Arrange:** Place the grilled meat and vegetables on a serving platter.
   - **Accompaniments:** Serve with steamed white rice, pickled vegetables, and fresh greens. Offer the yakiniku sauce for dipping or drizzling over the meat.
   - **Garnish:** Garnish with sliced green onions, sesame seeds, and any additional toppings.

Notes:

- **Meat Quality:** The key to great yakiniku is high-quality meat. Choose well-marbled cuts for the best flavor and tenderness.
- **Marinating:** Marinating adds extra flavor, but if you're short on time, you can grill the meat directly with simple seasoning.
- **Sauce Variations:** Feel free to adjust the yakiniku sauce to suit your taste. You can add more garlic, ginger, or spices according to your preference.
- **Grilling Alternatives:** If you don't have a grill, you can use a broiler or stovetop grill pan. Ensure good ventilation as grilling can produce smoke.

Yakiniku is a versatile and delicious dish that's perfect for both casual gatherings and special occasions. With its savory flavors and variety of accompaniments, it offers a great way to enjoy grilled meat in a flavorful and satisfying way. Enjoy your yakiniku meal!

Okonomiyaki

Ingredients:

For the Batter:

- 1 cup all-purpose flour
- 2/3 cup dashi stock (or water)
- 2 large eggs
- 1 tablespoon soy sauce
- 1 tablespoon mirin (sweet rice wine)
- 1/4 teaspoon salt
- 1/2 teaspoon baking powder

For the Filling:

- 2 cups shredded cabbage
- 1/2 cup thinly sliced green onions
- 1/2 cup cooked and chopped bacon or pork belly (or substitute with seafood like shrimp or squid)
- 1/4 cup grated carrots (optional)
- 1/4 cup pickled ginger, chopped (optional)
- 1/2 cup shredded cheese (optional)

For Toppings:

- Okonomiyaki sauce (store-bought or homemade, see recipe below)
- Japanese mayonnaise
- Bonito flakes (katsuobushi)
- Aonori (dried seaweed flakes)
- Thinly sliced green onions

For Homemade Okonomiyaki Sauce (Optional):

- 1/4 cup Worcestershire sauce
- 2 tablespoons ketchup
- 1 tablespoon soy sauce
- 1 tablespoon mirin
- 1 tablespoon sugar

Instructions:

1. **Prepare the Batter:**

- **Mix Ingredients:** In a large bowl, whisk together the flour, dashi stock (or water), eggs, soy sauce, mirin, salt, and baking powder until smooth.
2. **Add Fillings:**
   - **Combine:** Fold in shredded cabbage, green onions, bacon (or your choice of meat/seafood), carrots, pickled ginger, and cheese if using.
3. **Cook the Okonomiyaki:**
   - **Preheat the Pan:** Heat a griddle or non-stick skillet over medium heat and lightly grease it with oil.
   - **Pour the Batter:** Pour a portion of the batter onto the griddle, spreading it into a circle about 1/2 inch thick. Use a spatula to shape it into an even, round pancake.
   - **Cook:** Cook for about 4-5 minutes until the bottom is golden brown and crispy. Flip carefully and cook the other side for another 4-5 minutes, or until cooked through and golden brown.
4. **Prepare Toppings:**
   - **Make Sauce (Optional):** For homemade okonomiyaki sauce, combine Worcestershire sauce, ketchup, soy sauce, mirin, and sugar in a small bowl. Adjust to taste and set aside.
5. **Serve:**
   - **Top and Garnish:** Once the okonomiyaki is cooked, transfer it to a plate. Drizzle with okonomiyaki sauce and Japanese mayonnaise. Sprinkle with bonito flakes, aonori, and sliced green onions.
   - **Cut and Enjoy:** Slice into wedges and serve hot.

Notes:

- **Fillings:** The beauty of okonomiyaki lies in its flexibility. Feel free to add or substitute ingredients based on your preferences, such as adding mushrooms, seafood, or different types of meat.
- **Cooking:** Be patient while cooking. Ensure that the pancake is cooked through by checking that both sides are golden brown and the center is set.
- **Garnishes:** Okonomiyaki sauce and Japanese mayonnaise are essential for the authentic flavor, but you can adjust the amount to your taste.
- **Pan Choice:** A cast-iron skillet or griddle works well for achieving a crispy crust. If you don't have one, a non-stick pan is a good alternative.

Okonomiyaki is a fun and customizable dish that allows you to experiment with different ingredients and flavors. It's perfect for a casual meal or a gathering with friends and family. Enjoy making and eating this delicious Japanese pancake!

Takoyaki

Ingredients:

For the Takoyaki Batter:

- 1 cup all-purpose flour
- 1 1/2 cups dashi stock (or water if dashi is unavailable)
- 2 large eggs
- 1/4 teaspoon salt
- 1/4 teaspoon soy sauce
- 1/4 teaspoon sugar

For the Filling:

- 1 cup cooked octopus, chopped into small pieces (substitute with shrimp or chicken if desired)
- 1/4 cup pickled ginger, chopped
- 1/4 cup green onions, finely chopped
- 1/4 cup tempura scraps (tenkasu), optional for added texture

For Toppings:

- Takoyaki sauce (store-bought or homemade, see recipe below)
- Japanese mayonnaise
- Bonito flakes (katsuobushi)
- Aonori (dried seaweed flakes)
- Pickled ginger (for garnish)
- Sliced green onions

For Homemade Takoyaki Sauce (Optional):

- 1/4 cup Worcestershire sauce
- 2 tablespoons ketchup
- 1 tablespoon soy sauce
- 1 tablespoon mirin
- 1 tablespoon sugar

Instructions:

1. **Prepare the Takoyaki Batter:**
    - **Mix Ingredients:** In a large bowl, whisk together flour, dashi stock (or water), eggs, salt, soy sauce, and sugar until smooth. Set aside.
2. **Prepare the Takoyaki Filling:**

- **Combine Ingredients:** In a small bowl, mix together chopped octopus, pickled ginger, green onions, and tempura scraps (if using).
3. **Heat the Takoyaki Pan:**
    - **Preheat:** Place a takoyaki pan (or special takoyaki grill) over medium heat. Lightly oil each of the holes using a brush or a paper towel dipped in oil.
4. **Cook the Takoyaki:**
    - **Pour Batter:** Fill each hole in the takoyaki pan with batter, about 3/4 full.
    - **Add Filling:** Place a small amount of the octopus mixture into each hole.
    - **Cook:** Allow the batter to cook for a few minutes until it starts to set around the edges. Use a skewer or chopsticks to gently turn each takoyaki ball, rotating it 90 degrees to cook evenly on all sides. Continue cooking and rotating until the takoyaki balls are golden brown and crispy on the outside, about 6-8 minutes.
5. **Prepare Toppings:**
    - **Make Sauce (Optional):** For homemade takoyaki sauce, combine Worcestershire sauce, ketchup, soy sauce, mirin, and sugar in a small bowl. Adjust to taste.
6. **Serve:**
    - **Top and Garnish:** Transfer the takoyaki balls to a serving plate. Drizzle with takoyaki sauce and Japanese mayonnaise. Sprinkle with bonito flakes, aonori, and extra pickled ginger and green onions if desired.
    - **Enjoy:** Serve hot, and enjoy!

Notes:

- **Takoyaki Pan:** A special takoyaki pan is ideal for making evenly shaped takoyaki balls. If you don't have one, you can use a similar pan with small, rounded indentations or even try using a mini muffin tin, though results may vary.
- **Batter Consistency:** The batter should be pourable but not too runny. It should flow easily into the holes of the takoyaki pan.
- **Fillings:** Traditional takoyaki uses octopus, but you can get creative with other fillings like cooked shrimp, cheese, or even vegetables.
- **Cooking Technique:** Rotating the takoyaki balls as they cook ensures they develop a round shape and crispy exterior. It can be a bit tricky at first, so practice makes perfect!

Takoyaki is a fun and interactive dish that's great for parties and gatherings. Its savory and slightly sweet flavor, combined with various toppings, makes it a delicious and satisfying treat. Enjoy making and eating this classic Japanese street food!

Katsu Curry

Ingredients:

For the Pork Katsu:

- 4 boneless pork loin or pork chop cutlets (about 1/2-inch thick)
- Salt and pepper, to taste
- 1/2 cup all-purpose flour
- 2 large eggs
- 1 cup panko breadcrumbs
- Vegetable oil, for frying

For the Curry Sauce:

- 2 tablespoons vegetable oil
- 1 large onion, finely chopped
- 2 cloves garlic, minced
- 1 tablespoon ginger, minced
- 2 medium carrots, peeled and diced
- 2 medium potatoes, peeled and diced
- 3 cups chicken or vegetable broth
- 1-2 tablespoons curry powder (adjust to taste)
- 1-2 tablespoons soy sauce (optional)
- 1-2 tablespoons sugar (optional)
- 1-2 tablespoons soy sauce (optional)
- 1 tablespoon cornstarch mixed with 2 tablespoons water (optional, for thickening)

For Serving:

- Steamed white rice
- Pickled vegetables (optional)

Instructions:

1. **Prepare the Pork Katsu:**
    - **Season the Pork:** Season the pork cutlets with salt and pepper.
    - **Breading Station:** Set up a breading station with three shallow dishes. Place flour in the first dish, beaten eggs in the second, and panko breadcrumbs in the third.
    - **Coat the Pork:** Dredge each pork cutlet in flour, shaking off excess. Dip into the beaten eggs, then coat thoroughly with panko breadcrumbs.
    - **Fry the Katsu:** Heat vegetable oil in a large skillet over medium-high heat. Fry the breaded pork cutlets for about 4-5 minutes per side, or until golden brown

and cooked through. Drain on paper towels and keep warm. Slice into strips before serving.

2. **Prepare the Curry Sauce:**
   - **Sauté Aromatics:** Heat vegetable oil in a large saucepan or skillet over medium heat. Add onions and cook until softened and translucent, about 5 minutes. Add garlic and ginger and cook for another minute until fragrant.
   - **Cook Vegetables:** Add carrots and potatoes and cook for 5 minutes, stirring occasionally.
   - **Add Broth and Spices:** Pour in the chicken or vegetable broth and bring to a boil. Reduce heat and let it simmer for about 15 minutes, or until vegetables are tender.
   - **Season the Curry:** Stir in curry powder, adjusting the amount to taste. If desired, add soy sauce and sugar to balance the flavors.
   - **Thicken (Optional):** If you prefer a thicker sauce, stir in the cornstarch mixture and cook until the sauce has thickened to your liking.

3. **Serve:**
   - **Plate the Rice:** Place a portion of steamed white rice on each plate.
   - **Add the Curry Sauce:** Spoon the curry sauce over the rice.
   - **Top with Katsu:** Arrange slices of pork katsu on top of the curry sauce.
   - **Garnish:** Optionally, serve with pickled vegetables on the side.

Notes:

- **Rice:** Short-grain or medium-grain rice works best for this dish due to its sticky texture, which complements the curry sauce.
- **Curry Powder:** Japanese curry powder is typically milder and sweeter than other types of curry powder. Adjust the amount based on your preference for spiciness.
- **Katsu Variations:** While pork katsu is traditional, you can substitute with chicken katsu or even tofu for a vegetarian option.
- **Thickening:** The curry sauce can be adjusted for thickness. If you prefer a smoother, thicker sauce, the cornstarch mixture helps achieve that consistency.

Katsu Curry is a comforting and flavorful dish that combines the best elements of crispy katsu with a rich, savory curry sauce. It's a hearty meal that's sure to satisfy your taste buds. Enjoy making and savoring this delicious Japanese favorite!

Yuba (Tofu Skin) Salad

Ingredients:

For the Salad:

- 100g (3.5 oz) yuba (tofu skin), soaked in warm water until softened
- 1 cucumber, thinly sliced
- 1 small carrot, julienned
- 1 cup cherry tomatoes, halved
- 1/4 cup radishes, thinly sliced
- 1/4 cup fresh cilantro or shiso leaves, chopped
- 1 avocado, sliced (optional)

For the Dressing:

- 2 tablespoons soy sauce
- 1 tablespoon rice vinegar
- 1 tablespoon sesame oil
- 1 teaspoon honey or sugar (adjust to taste)
- 1 clove garlic, minced
- 1 teaspoon grated ginger
- 1 teaspoon sesame seeds (optional)
- 1 teaspoon toasted sesame seeds (optional)

Instructions:

1. **Prepare the Yuba:**
    - **Soak the Yuba:** If using dried yuba, soak it in warm water according to package instructions until softened. Drain well and pat dry with paper towels. If using fresh yuba, rinse and drain it well.
2. **Prepare the Vegetables:**
    - **Slice and Julienne:** Thinly slice the cucumber and radishes. Julienne the carrot. Halve the cherry tomatoes. Slice the avocado if using.
3. **Prepare the Dressing:**
    - **Mix Ingredients:** In a small bowl, whisk together soy sauce, rice vinegar, sesame oil, honey or sugar, minced garlic, and grated ginger. Adjust the sweetness or acidity to taste. Optionally, add sesame seeds for extra flavor.
4. **Assemble the Salad:**
    - **Combine:** In a large salad bowl, combine the softened yuba, cucumber, carrot, cherry tomatoes, radishes, and cilantro or shiso leaves. Gently toss to mix.
    - **Dress the Salad:** Drizzle the prepared dressing over the salad and toss gently to coat all ingredients.
5. **Serve:**
    - **Garnish and Serve:** Top the salad with avocado slices if using and additional sesame seeds if desired. Serve immediately.

Notes:

- **Yuba Types:** Yuba comes in different forms, such as fresh, dried, or frozen. The soaking time will vary depending on the type you use. Fresh yuba is more delicate and requires less preparation.
- **Vegetable Variations:** Feel free to add other vegetables like bell peppers, edamame, or shredded cabbage to suit your taste.
- **Dressing Adjustments:** You can adjust the dressing ingredients to suit your preference. For a spicier kick, add a dash of chili oil or a pinch of red pepper flakes.
- **Serving:** Yuba salad is best served fresh, but you can prepare the components ahead of time and mix just before serving to keep the vegetables crisp.

Yuba Salad is a light, nutritious, and versatile dish that's perfect for a healthy lunch or as a side dish. Its combination of fresh vegetables, delicate tofu skin, and a flavorful dressing makes it a refreshing addition to any meal. Enjoy this elegant and wholesome salad!

Tonkotsu Ramen

Ingredients:

For the Tonkotsu Broth:

- 2 lbs (900g) pork bones (preferably with a bit of meat attached)
- 1 lb (450g) pork feet or pork neck bones (optional, for richer flavor)
- 1 onion, peeled and halved
- 1 head garlic, halved
- 2-inch piece of ginger, sliced
- 1 leek or 2 green onions, chopped (optional)
- Water (enough to cover the bones)

For the Tare (Seasoning Sauce):

- 1/4 cup soy sauce
- 2 tablespoons miso paste
- 2 tablespoons sake (Japanese rice wine)
- 1 tablespoon mirin (sweet rice wine)
- 1 teaspoon sugar

For the Toppings:

- 4 servings of ramen noodles
- 4 slices of chashu pork (braised pork belly)
- 4 soft-boiled eggs (marinated or plain)
- 1 cup bamboo shoots (menma)
- 1 cup sliced green onions
- 1 cup mushrooms (shiitake or enoki), optional
- 1 sheet nori (seaweed), cut into strips
- Bean sprouts or corn, optional
- Fresh cilantro or shiso leaves, for garnish

Instructions:

1. **Prepare the Broth:**
    - **Blanch the Bones:** Place pork bones and optional pork feet in a large pot of cold water. Bring to a boil and then discard the water. Rinse the bones under cold running water to remove impurities.
    - **Simmer:** In a clean pot, add the blanched bones, onion, garlic, ginger, and leek (if using). Cover with fresh water and bring to a boil. Reduce the heat to a simmer and cook for at least 6-8 hours, skimming off any foam or impurities that rise to

the surface. The longer you simmer, the richer and creamier the broth will be. Add more water as needed to keep the bones covered.
    - **Strain:** After simmering, strain the broth through a fine-mesh sieve or cheesecloth into a clean pot. Discard the solids and return the strained broth to the pot.
2. **Prepare the Tare:**
    - **Mix Ingredients:** In a small bowl, combine soy sauce, miso paste, sake, mirin, and sugar. Stir until the miso is fully dissolved. Adjust the seasoning to taste if necessary.
3. **Cook the Noodles:**
    - **Boil:** Cook the ramen noodles according to the package instructions. Drain and rinse under cold water to stop the cooking process. Set aside.
4. **Prepare the Toppings:**
    - **Chashu Pork:** If you have pre-made chashu pork, slice it thinly. If making your own, braise pork belly until tender and slice.
    - **Soft-Boiled Eggs:** Marinate or cook the eggs to your preference. For a marinated egg, soak in soy sauce and mirin mixture for a few hours.
    - **Mushrooms and Vegetables:** If using mushrooms or additional vegetables, sauté or prepare them as desired.
5. **Assemble the Ramen:**
    - **Season the Broth:** Add a few tablespoons of the tare mixture to the hot broth and stir well. Adjust the seasoning to taste.
    - **Serve:** Place a portion of cooked ramen noodles into each bowl. Ladle the hot broth over the noodles. Top with chashu pork, soft-boiled egg, bamboo shoots, green onions, mushrooms, nori, and any other desired toppings.
    - **Garnish:** Add fresh cilantro or shiso leaves if desired.
6. **Enjoy:**
    - **Serve Immediately:** Tonkotsu ramen is best enjoyed hot. Serve immediately and enjoy!

Notes:

- **Broth Richness:** For an ultra-rich broth, you can continue simmering the bones for up to 12-14 hours. Some recipes even use a pressure cooker to speed up the process.
- **Tare Adjustments:** The tare is a key component in achieving the perfect balance of flavors. Adjust the quantities of soy sauce, miso, and sugar to suit your taste preferences.
- **Chashu Pork:** Chashu pork can be made ahead of time and kept in the refrigerator. It's often braised for several hours to become tender and flavorful.
- **Noodle Texture:** Ramen noodles should be cooked just before serving to ensure they remain firm and don't become mushy in the broth.

Tonkotsu Ramen is a deeply flavorful and comforting dish that brings together the richness of pork bone broth with the savory elements of Japanese cuisine. Enjoy the process of making this classic ramen and savor every bowl of homemade goodness!

Ebi Fry (Fried Shrimp)

Ingredients:

For the Shrimp:

- 12 large shrimp (peeled, deveined, and tails left on)
- Salt and pepper, to taste
- 1/2 cup all-purpose flour
- 2 large eggs
- 1 cup panko breadcrumbs
- Vegetable oil, for frying

For the Dipping Sauce:

- 1/4 cup ketchup
- 2 tablespoons Worcestershire sauce
- 1 tablespoon soy sauce
- 1 tablespoon mirin (sweet rice wine) or honey
- 1 teaspoon Dijon mustard (optional)
- 1 teaspoon grated ginger (optional)

For Serving:

- Lemon wedges
- Shredded cabbage (optional)
- Rice or miso soup (optional)

Instructions:

1. **Prepare the Shrimp:**
    - **Season:** Pat the shrimp dry with paper towels and season lightly with salt and pepper.
    - **Set Up Breading Station:** Set up a breading station with three shallow dishes: one with flour, one with beaten eggs, and one with panko breadcrumbs.
2. **Bread the Shrimp:**
    - **Dredge:** Dredge each shrimp in flour, shaking off any excess.
    - **Dip:** Dip the floured shrimp into the beaten eggs, allowing any excess to drip off.
    - **Coat:** Coat the shrimp with panko breadcrumbs, pressing lightly to ensure the breadcrumbs adhere well. Set aside on a plate.
3. **Prepare the Dipping Sauce:**
    - **Mix Ingredients:** In a small bowl, combine ketchup, Worcestershire sauce, soy sauce, mirin or honey, and Dijon mustard and grated ginger if using. Stir until well combined. Adjust seasoning to taste.

4. **Fry the Shrimp:**
    - **Heat Oil:** In a large skillet or deep fryer, heat vegetable oil to 350°F (175°C). You need enough oil to submerge the shrimp halfway, about 2 inches deep.
    - **Fry:** Carefully add the shrimp to the hot oil in batches, avoiding overcrowding. Fry for 2-3 minutes on each side, or until golden brown and crispy. Remove with a slotted spoon and drain on paper towels.
5. **Serve:**
    - **Garnish and Serve:** Serve the ebi fry hot with lemon wedges for squeezing over the shrimp. Optionally, serve with shredded cabbage, rice, or miso soup on the side.

Notes:

- **Shrimp Size:** Large shrimp work best for this recipe. Ensure they are thoroughly dried before breading to help the coating stick better.
- **Oil Temperature:** Maintain a consistent oil temperature to ensure that the shrimp cook evenly and achieve a crispy coating.
- **Variations:** For a different flavor, you can mix some finely grated Parmesan cheese into the panko breadcrumbs or add a pinch of cayenne pepper for a bit of heat.
- **Serving Suggestions:** Ebi fry is often served with a side of shredded cabbage dressed with a light vinaigrette, but it can also be enjoyed as a topping for salads or alongside other Japanese dishes.

Ebi Fry is a delightful and crispy treat that's perfect for a quick meal or as a delicious appetizer. Enjoy the satisfying crunch and tender shrimp of this classic Japanese favorite!

Soba Noodles with Dipping Sauce

Ingredients:

For the Soba Noodles:

- 8 oz (225g) soba noodles (buckwheat noodles)
- Water, for boiling

For the Dipping Sauce (Tsuyu):

- 1/2 cup soy sauce
- 1/4 cup mirin (sweet rice wine)
- 1/4 cup dashi stock (or substitute with water for a milder flavor)
- 1 tablespoon sugar (optional)
- 1 teaspoon grated ginger (optional)
- 1 teaspoon sesame seeds (optional)

For Garnishing (Optional):

- 1-2 green onions, thinly sliced
- Wasabi or horseradish (to taste)
- Pickled ginger
- Nori (seaweed) sheets, cut into strips
- Shredded daikon radish

Instructions:

1. **Prepare the Soba Noodles:**
   - **Boil Noodles:** Bring a large pot of water to a boil. Add the soba noodles and cook according to package instructions, usually for about 4-6 minutes, until just tender but still firm to the bite.
   - **Cool Noodles:** Drain the noodles and rinse under cold running water to stop the cooking process and cool them down. Drain thoroughly and set aside.
2. **Prepare the Dipping Sauce:**
   - **Combine Ingredients:** In a small saucepan, combine soy sauce, mirin, dashi stock, and sugar (if using). Bring to a simmer over medium heat, stirring occasionally until the sugar dissolves. Remove from heat and let cool.
   - **Add Ginger and Sesame Seeds:** If using, stir in grated ginger and sesame seeds. Adjust seasoning to taste if necessary.
3. **Serve:**
   - **Assemble:** Divide the chilled soba noodles among serving plates or bowls.
   - **Dipping Sauce:** Pour the cooled dipping sauce into small dipping bowls, one for each person.

- **Garnish:** Garnish with optional toppings like sliced green onions, wasabi, pickled ginger, nori strips, or shredded daikon radish.

4. **Enjoy:**
   - **Dip and Eat:** To eat, dip a small portion of soba noodles into the dipping sauce and enjoy. You can also add some of the garnishes directly into the dipping sauce for added flavor.

Notes:

- **Dashi Stock:** Traditional dashi stock is made from dried bonito flakes and kombu (sea kelp). You can use instant dashi powder or substitute with vegetable or chicken broth if dashi is not available.
- **Noodle Cooking:** Avoid overcooking the soba noodles; they should have a slight bite to them. Rinsing under cold water helps to remove excess starch and keep the noodles from sticking together.
- **Variations:** This dish can be adapted with additional toppings such as tempura vegetables, cooked shrimp, or fresh herbs to suit your taste.
- **Storage:** Soba noodles can be stored in the refrigerator for a day or two after cooking, but they are best enjoyed fresh. If storing, keep the noodles and dipping sauce separate until ready to serve.

Soba Noodles with Dipping Sauce is a versatile and refreshing dish that highlights the unique flavor of buckwheat noodles. It's perfect for a light meal or as part of a larger Japanese meal. Enjoy the simplicity and elegance of this classic Japanese dish!

Nabe (Hot Pot)

Ingredients:

For the Broth:

- 4 cups dashi stock (or use chicken or vegetable broth as an alternative)
- 1/4 cup soy sauce
- 2 tablespoons mirin (sweet rice wine)
- 1 tablespoon sake (Japanese rice wine)
- 1-2 tablespoons miso paste (optional, for a miso nabe)

For the Hot Pot Ingredients:

- 1/2 lb (225g) thinly sliced beef, pork, or chicken (or a mix)
- 1 cup shiitake mushrooms, sliced
- 1 cup enoki mushrooms
- 1 cup baby bok choy or spinach
- 1 medium carrot, sliced thinly
- 1 cup tofu, cut into cubes
- 1 cup napa cabbage, chopped
- 1 cup udon noodles or soba noodles (optional)
- 1/2 cup scallions, chopped
- 1/2 cup bamboo shoots or water chestnuts (optional)

For Serving:

- Cooked rice
- Soy sauce
- Sesame oil
- Pickled ginger or kimchi (optional)

Instructions:

1. **Prepare the Broth:**
   - **Combine Ingredients:** In a large pot or nabe pot, combine the dashi stock, soy sauce, mirin, and sake. If using miso paste, dissolve it in a small amount of hot broth and then add it to the pot.
   - **Simmer:** Bring the broth to a simmer over medium heat. Adjust seasoning to taste if needed.
2. **Prepare the Ingredients:**
   - **Slice and Chop:** Slice the meat thinly if it's not pre-sliced. Prepare all vegetables, mushrooms, tofu, and noodles as indicated.

- - **Arrange:** Arrange the ingredients on a platter or in bowls for easy access during the meal.
3. **Cook the Hot Pot:**
    - **Heat:** Bring the broth to a gentle simmer at the table over a portable burner.
    - **Cook:** Add the ingredients to the simmering broth as desired. Start with items that take longer to cook, such as the meat and root vegetables, and then add quicker-cooking ingredients like mushrooms, tofu, and greens.
    - **Cook Noodles:** If using noodles, add them to the pot towards the end of cooking.
4. **Serve:**
    - **Customize:** Each person can select their desired ingredients from the pot and place them into their bowl.
    - **Enjoy:** Ladle some of the broth over the cooked ingredients in each bowl. Serve with cooked rice and additional condiments like soy sauce, sesame oil, or pickled ginger if desired.

Notes:

- **Dashi Stock:** Dashi is a traditional Japanese stock made from dried bonito flakes and kombu. You can use store-bought dashi powder or make it from scratch.
- **Meat and Protein:** Thinly sliced meat is commonly used in nabe. You can also use seafood or other proteins based on preference.
- **Vegetable Variations:** Feel free to add other vegetables like bell peppers, corn, or sweet potatoes according to your taste.
- **Serving Style:** Nabe is typically enjoyed communally at the table, with everyone adding and cooking ingredients in the pot as they eat. This creates a fun and interactive dining experience.
- **Broth Variations:** There are many types of nabe, including miso nabe, shabu-shabu (which uses a different broth and dipping sauces), and sukiyaki. Adjust the broth ingredients to suit the type of nabe you prefer.

Nabe is a versatile and heartwarming dish perfect for gatherings, as it brings people together around a bubbling pot of delicious, customizable ingredients. Enjoy the interactive and cozy nature of this traditional Japanese hot pot!

Hiyayakko (Cold Tofu)

Ingredients:

- 1 block of silken tofu (about 14 oz or 400g)
- 2 tablespoons soy sauce
- 1 teaspoon mirin (sweet rice wine) or honey
- 1 teaspoon rice vinegar or lemon juice
- 1 tablespoon grated fresh ginger (optional)
- 2 green onions, finely sliced
- 1 tablespoon bonito flakes (katsuobushi), optional
- 1 teaspoon sesame seeds (optional)
- A small handful of shiso leaves or parsley for garnish (optional)

Instructions:

1. **Prepare the Tofu:**
   - **Drain:** Carefully remove the tofu from its package and drain off any excess liquid.
   - **Chill:** Place the tofu on a plate or serving dish. For best results, refrigerate the tofu for at least 30 minutes to ensure it's cold and firm.
2. **Prepare the Sauce:**
   - **Mix Ingredients:** In a small bowl, combine soy sauce, mirin or honey, and rice vinegar or lemon juice. Stir until well mixed. Adjust seasoning to taste if necessary.
3. **Assemble the Dish:**
   - **Top Tofu:** Just before serving, cut the chilled tofu into squares or slices if it's not already pre-cut. Drizzle the prepared sauce over the tofu.
   - **Add Toppings:** Sprinkle the tofu with grated ginger (if using), sliced green onions, bonito flakes, sesame seeds, and garnish with shiso leaves or parsley if desired.
4. **Serve:**
   - **Enjoy:** Serve the hiyayakko immediately as a refreshing side dish or light appetizer. It pairs well with rice and other Japanese dishes.

Notes:

- **Tofu Type:** Silken tofu is ideal for this dish due to its smooth, creamy texture. If using firmer tofu, press it to remove excess moisture and chill it before serving.
- **Garnishes:** You can customize the toppings based on your preference. Common variations include adding finely chopped cucumber, radish, or even a drizzle of sesame oil.
- **Sauce Adjustments:** The sauce can be adjusted to taste. For a richer flavor, you might add a splash of dashi stock or a bit of grated daikon radish.
- **Chilled Tofu:** The tofu should be thoroughly chilled for the best texture and flavor. If preparing in advance, keep it covered in the refrigerator until ready to serve.

Hiyayakko is a minimalist dish that highlights the delicate flavor of tofu while allowing for a variety of optional toppings. It's a perfect addition to a summer meal or as a refreshing complement to other Japanese dishes. Enjoy the simplicity and freshness of this classic Japanese favorite!

Ebi Chili

Ingredients:

For the Shrimp:

- 1 lb (450g) large shrimp, peeled and deveined
- 1 tablespoon cornstarch
- 1 tablespoon vegetable oil (for sautéing)

For the Chili Sauce:

- 2 tablespoons vegetable oil
- 1 onion, finely chopped
- 2 cloves garlic, minced
- 1-inch piece of ginger, minced
- 1-2 tablespoons chili paste or sauce (adjust to taste)
- 1 tablespoon soy sauce
- 2 tablespoons rice vinegar
- 2 tablespoons sugar (or honey)
- 1/2 cup chicken or vegetable broth
- 1 tablespoon ketchup (optional, for a touch of sweetness)
- 1 tablespoon cornstarch mixed with 2 tablespoons water (for thickening)

For Garnishing:

- 2 green onions, sliced
- Sesame seeds (optional)
- Fresh cilantro or parsley (optional)

Instructions:

1. **Prepare the Shrimp:**
   - **Coat Shrimp:** Toss the peeled and deveined shrimp with cornstarch until they are evenly coated.
   - **Cook Shrimp:** Heat vegetable oil in a large skillet or wok over medium-high heat. Add the shrimp and cook for 2-3 minutes on each side, or until pink and cooked through. Remove the shrimp from the skillet and set aside.
2. **Prepare the Chili Sauce:**
   - **Sauté Aromatics:** In the same skillet, add vegetable oil and sauté the chopped onion until translucent and slightly golden.
   - **Add Garlic and Ginger:** Stir in the minced garlic and ginger, cooking for another minute until fragrant.
   - **Add Chili Paste:** Add the chili paste or sauce to the skillet and cook for 1-2 minutes, stirring constantly.
   - **Add Sauce Ingredients:** Stir in the soy sauce, rice vinegar, sugar, and chicken or vegetable broth. Mix well and bring the sauce to a simmer.

- **Thicken Sauce:** Add the cornstarch-water mixture to the simmering sauce, stirring constantly until the sauce thickens to your desired consistency.
3. **Combine and Cook:**
    - **Add Shrimp:** Return the cooked shrimp to the skillet and toss to coat them with the chili sauce. Cook for an additional 1-2 minutes until the shrimp are heated through and well coated with the sauce.
4. **Serve:**
    - **Garnish:** Transfer the ebi chili to a serving dish and garnish with sliced green onions, sesame seeds, and fresh cilantro or parsley if desired.
    - **Accompany:** Serve hot with steamed rice or noodles.

Notes:

- **Chili Paste:** You can use Chinese chili bean paste (doubanjiang) or other chili sauces depending on your heat preference and availability. Adjust the amount based on how spicy you like your dish.
- **Sweetness Balance:** Adjust the sugar or honey to balance the spiciness of the sauce. You can add more or less depending on your taste preference.
- **Thickening Sauce:** If the sauce is too thick, add a little more broth to reach your desired consistency. If it's too thin, let it simmer a bit longer to reduce and thicken further.
- **Vegetable Variations:** Feel free to add vegetables like bell peppers, snap peas, or broccoli to the dish for added texture and flavor.

Ebi Chili is a deliciously spicy and sweet shrimp dish that's perfect for a quick weeknight dinner or a special occasion. Enjoy the balance of flavors and the satisfying bite of shrimp in this classic Japanese favorite!

Miso Glazed Black Cod

Ingredients:

For the Miso Marinade:

- 1/2 cup white miso paste
- 1/4 cup sake (Japanese rice wine)
- 1/4 cup mirin (sweet rice wine)
- 3 tablespoons sugar
- 1 tablespoon soy sauce

For the Black Cod:

- 4 black cod fillets (about 6 oz or 170g each)
- 1 tablespoon vegetable oil (for cooking)

For Garnishing:

- Sliced green onions
- Sesame seeds
- Lemon wedges (optional)

Instructions:

1. **Prepare the Marinade:**
   - **Combine Ingredients:** In a small saucepan, combine white miso paste, sake, mirin, sugar, and soy sauce.
   - **Heat and Stir:** Bring the mixture to a simmer over medium heat, stirring continuously until the sugar dissolves and the sauce is smooth. Remove from heat and let cool to room temperature.
2. **Marinate the Cod:**
   - **Prepare Fillets:** Pat the black cod fillets dry with paper towels.
   - **Marinate:** Place the fillets in a resealable plastic bag or shallow dish. Pour the cooled miso marinade over the fillets, ensuring they are well coated. Seal the bag or cover the dish and refrigerate for at least 2 hours, preferably overnight for best flavor.
3. **Cook the Cod:**
   - **Preheat Oven:** Preheat your oven to 400°F (200°C).
   - **Prepare Baking Sheet:** Line a baking sheet with parchment paper or lightly grease it with vegetable oil.
   - **Bake:** Remove the fillets from the marinade and shake off any excess. Place the fillets on the prepared baking sheet. Bake for 12-15 minutes, or until the fish is opaque and flakes easily with a fork. The surface should be caramelized and slightly golden.
4. **Serve:**
   - **Garnish:** Transfer the cooked black cod to serving plates. Garnish with sliced green onions, sesame seeds, and lemon wedges if desired.

- **Accompany:** Serve with steamed rice and sautéed vegetables or a fresh salad for a complete meal.

Notes:

- **Miso Paste:** White miso paste is milder and sweeter compared to red miso, making it ideal for this dish. If using red miso, you might want to adjust the sugar and marinade to balance the stronger flavor.
- **Marinating Time:** For the best results, allow the cod to marinate for at least 2 hours, but overnight is preferable to let the flavors penetrate the fish deeply.
- **Cooking Method:** If you prefer, you can also broil the cod for a few minutes at the end of cooking to achieve a more caramelized surface.
- **Substitution:** If black cod is not available, you can use other fatty fish like salmon, but the texture and flavor may vary slightly.

Miso Glazed Black Cod is a luxurious and flavorful dish that showcases the delicate, buttery texture of the cod. The sweet and savory miso glaze makes it a standout meal that's perfect for special occasions or a refined weeknight dinner. Enjoy the deep umami flavors and tender fish in this classic Japanese recipe!

Japanese Style Fried Rice

Ingredients:

- **For the Fried Rice:**
    - 2 cups cooked and cooled rice (preferably day-old rice)
    - 2 tablespoons vegetable oil
    - 1 small onion, finely chopped
    - 2 cloves garlic, minced
    - 1 medium carrot, diced
    - 1 cup frozen peas
    - 1/2 cup cooked ham, bacon, or chicken, diced
    - 2 large eggs, lightly beaten
    - 2 green onions, sliced
    - 1-2 tablespoons soy sauce (adjust to taste)
    - 1 tablespoon oyster sauce (optional)
    - 1 teaspoon sesame oil
    - Salt and pepper to taste
- **For Garnishing (Optional):**
    - Pickled ginger
    - Extra green onions
    - Sesame seeds

Instructions:

1. **Prepare the Ingredients:**
    - **Rice:** Ensure your rice is cold and has been refrigerated. Freshly cooked rice can be too sticky and might not fry well.
    - **Chop Vegetables:** Dice the onion, carrot, and any other vegetables you plan to use. Chop the protein (ham, chicken, etc.) into small pieces.
2. **Cook the Fried Rice:**
    - **Heat Oil:** In a large skillet or wok, heat 2 tablespoons of vegetable oil over medium-high heat.
    - **Sauté Aromatics:** Add the chopped onion and cook for 2-3 minutes until translucent. Stir in the garlic and cook for an additional 30 seconds until fragrant.
    - **Add Vegetables and Protein:** Add the diced carrot and cook for 2 minutes. Add the frozen peas and diced ham, bacon, or chicken, and cook until heated through.
    - **Scramble Eggs:** Push the vegetables and protein to one side of the skillet. Pour the beaten eggs into the empty side of the skillet and scramble until cooked. Mix the eggs with the vegetables and protein.
3. **Fry the Rice:**
    - **Add Rice:** Add the cold rice to the skillet. Break up any clumps and stir to combine with the vegetables, protein, and eggs.
    - **Season:** Add soy sauce, oyster sauce (if using), and sesame oil. Stir-fry for 5-7 minutes, or until the rice is heated through and has a slightly crispy texture. Adjust seasoning with salt and pepper as needed.
4. **Finish and Serve:**
    - **Garnish:** Stir in the sliced green onions and remove from heat.

- **Serve:** Transfer the fried rice to serving plates. Garnish with pickled ginger, extra green onions, and sesame seeds if desired.

Notes:

- **Day-Old Rice:** Using rice that has been cooked and cooled in the refrigerator overnight helps to keep the grains separate and improves the texture of the fried rice. If using freshly cooked rice, spread it out on a baking sheet and let it cool for a while to reduce moisture.
- **Protein Choices:** You can use various proteins like shrimp, pork, or tofu instead of ham or chicken. Adjust cooking times accordingly to ensure the protein is fully cooked.
- **Vegetable Variations:** Feel free to customize with additional vegetables like bell peppers, mushrooms, or corn based on what you have available.
- **Heat:** Adjust the amount of soy sauce and seasoning to your taste. If you prefer a spicier version, you can add a dash of chili flakes or a splash of sriracha.

Japanese Style Fried Rice (Chahan) is a delightful dish that's easy to make and perfect for using up leftover rice. With its savory flavor and customizable ingredients, it's a great option for a quick, satisfying meal. Enjoy the simplicity and versatility of this classic Japanese favorite!

Gyudon (Beef Bowl)

Ingredients:

- **For the Beef Bowl:**

- 1 lb (450g) thinly sliced beef (such as sirloin or ribeye)
- 1 large onion, thinly sliced
- 2 tablespoons vegetable oil
- 1 cup dashi stock (or use beef or chicken broth)
- 1/4 cup soy sauce
- 2 tablespoons mirin (sweet rice wine)
- 2 tablespoons sugar
- 1 tablespoon sake (Japanese rice wine)
- 1 tablespoon cornstarch mixed with 1 tablespoon water (optional, for thickening)
- **For Serving:**
    - 4 cups steamed rice
    - Pickled ginger (beni shoga)
    - Sliced green onions
    - Shredded nori (seaweed) (optional)
    - Sesame seeds (optional)

Instructions:

1. **Prepare the Sauce:**
    - **Combine Ingredients:** In a large skillet or saucepan, heat 2 tablespoons of vegetable oil over medium heat.
    - **Cook Onions:** Add the thinly sliced onions and cook, stirring frequently, until they are softened and slightly caramelized, about 5 minutes.
    - **Add Beef:** Add the thinly sliced beef to the skillet and cook until it is no longer pink, stirring occasionally.
    - **Add Sauce Ingredients:** Pour in the dashi stock, soy sauce, mirin, sugar, and sake. Stir to combine and bring the mixture to a simmer.
2. **Simmer the Beef:**
    - **Cook:** Let the beef and onions simmer in the sauce for about 10 minutes, or until the beef is tender and the sauce has reduced slightly.
    - **Thicken Sauce (Optional):** If you prefer a thicker sauce, stir in the cornstarch-water mixture and cook for an additional 1-2 minutes until the sauce has thickened to your liking.
3. **Serve:**
    - **Prepare Rice:** Spoon steamed rice into serving bowls.
    - **Top with Beef:** Ladle the beef and onion mixture over the rice.
    - **Garnish:** Top with pickled ginger, sliced green onions, shredded nori, and sesame seeds if desired.

Notes:

- **Beef Choice:** Thinly sliced beef is ideal for gyudon. You can find pre-sliced beef at Asian grocery stores, or you can freeze a piece of beef slightly to make it easier to slice thinly yourself.

- **Dashi Stock:** Dashi is a traditional Japanese stock made from kombu (seaweed) and bonito flakes (dried fish). You can use store-bought dashi powder or substitute with beef or chicken broth if needed.
- **Rice:** Use short-grain or medium-grain rice for the best texture. Japanese rice or any sticky rice will work well for this dish.
- **Variations:** You can add other ingredients like mushrooms, bell peppers, or even a raw egg on top if you like.

Gyudon is a comforting and flavorful dish that's perfect for a quick and satisfying meal. Its combination of tender beef, sweet and savory sauce, and fluffy rice makes it a beloved classic in Japanese cuisine. Enjoy making and savoring this delicious beef bowl at home!

Chicken Teriyaki

Ingredients:

For the Teriyaki Sauce:

- 1/2 cup soy sauce
- 1/4 cup mirin (sweet rice wine)
- 1/4 cup sake (Japanese rice wine) or dry white wine
- 2 tablespoons sugar or honey
- 1 clove garlic, minced (optional)
- 1 teaspoon fresh ginger, minced (optional)

For the Chicken:

- 4 boneless, skinless chicken thighs (or breasts if preferred)
- 2 tablespoons vegetable oil
- Salt and pepper to taste
- 1 tablespoon cornstarch mixed with 1 tablespoon water (optional, for thickening)

For Serving:

- Steamed rice
- Steamed or stir-fried vegetables (such as broccoli, snap peas, or bell peppers)
- Sesame seeds (optional)
- Sliced green onions (optional)

Instructions:

1. **Prepare the Teriyaki Sauce:**
   - **Combine Ingredients:** In a small saucepan, combine soy sauce, mirin, sake, and sugar (or honey). Add minced garlic and ginger if using.
   - **Heat Sauce:** Bring the mixture to a simmer over medium heat, stirring occasionally. Simmer for 3-5 minutes until the sugar dissolves and the sauce slightly thickens. If you prefer a thicker sauce, stir in the cornstarch-water mixture and cook for an additional 1-2 minutes until thickened. Remove from heat and let cool.
2. **Prepare the Chicken:**
   - **Season Chicken:** Pat the chicken thighs dry with paper towels. Season both sides with salt and pepper.
   - **Cook Chicken:** Heat vegetable oil in a large skillet or grill pan over medium-high heat. Add the chicken thighs and cook for 5-7 minutes on each side, or until the chicken is fully cooked and has a nice golden-brown color. The internal temperature should reach 165°F (75°C).
   - **Glaze with Sauce:** Brush or pour a portion of the prepared teriyaki sauce over the chicken during the last few minutes of cooking. Continue cooking for another minute to let the sauce caramelize slightly. Reserve some sauce for serving.
3. **Serve:**

- **Slice Chicken:** Remove the chicken from the skillet or grill pan and let it rest for a few minutes. Slice the chicken into strips.
- **Plate:** Serve the sliced chicken over steamed rice. Drizzle with the remaining teriyaki sauce.
- **Garnish:** Garnish with sesame seeds and sliced green onions if desired. Serve with steamed or stir-fried vegetables on the side.

Notes:

- **Chicken Cuts:** Chicken thighs are preferred for their juiciness and flavor, but chicken breasts can also be used if you prefer a leaner option. Adjust cooking times as needed.
- **Marination:** For more flavor, you can marinate the chicken in a small amount of the teriyaki sauce for 30 minutes to a few hours before cooking.
- **Sauce Variations:** You can adjust the sweetness and saltiness of the sauce to your liking. If you like a stronger ginger flavor, increase the amount of minced ginger.
- **Serving Suggestions:** Chicken teriyaki pairs well with a variety of vegetables and can be served with a side of miso soup or a simple salad.

Chicken Teriyaki is a versatile and crowd-pleasing dish that's quick to prepare and full of flavor. Enjoy this classic Japanese recipe for a delicious and satisfying meal!

Spicy Tuna Don

Ingredients:

For the Spicy Tuna:

- 1/2 lb (225g) sushi-grade tuna, diced into small cubes
- 2 tablespoons mayonnaise (Japanese Kewpie mayo preferred)
- 1 tablespoon Sriracha sauce (adjust to taste)
- 1 teaspoon soy sauce
- 1 teaspoon sesame oil
- 1 teaspoon rice vinegar
- 1 teaspoon finely chopped green onions (optional)
- 1 teaspoon sesame seeds (optional)
- 1 avocado, diced (optional)

For the Rice Bowl:

- 2 cups steamed sushi rice or short-grain rice
- 1/2 cucumber, thinly sliced
- 1/2 cup shredded carrots
- 1 small radish, thinly sliced (optional)
- Pickled ginger (beni shoga) (optional)
- Seaweed strips or shredded nori (optional)

For Garnishing:

- Sliced green onions
- Sesame seeds
- Extra Sriracha sauce (for drizzling, optional)
- Soy sauce (for drizzling, optional)

Instructions:

1. **Prepare the Spicy Tuna:**
   - **Mix Ingredients:** In a bowl, combine the mayonnaise, Sriracha sauce, soy sauce, sesame oil, and rice vinegar. Mix well to make the spicy mayo sauce.
   - **Add Tuna:** Gently fold the diced tuna into the spicy mayo mixture until the tuna is well coated. If using, stir in the finely chopped green onions and diced avocado.
2. **Prepare the Rice Bowl:**
   - **Cook Rice:** If you haven't done so already, cook the sushi rice or short-grain rice according to the package instructions. Let it cool slightly before serving.
   - **Assemble Bowl:** Divide the cooked rice among serving bowls. Arrange the sliced cucumber, shredded carrots, and radish on top of the rice.
3. **Assemble and Serve:**
   - **Add Tuna:** Spoon the spicy tuna mixture over the rice and vegetables in each bowl.

- **Garnish:** Garnish with sliced green onions, sesame seeds, and additional Sriracha sauce if desired. Drizzle with soy sauce for extra flavor.
4. **Optional Toppings:**
    - **Pickled Ginger:** Add pickled ginger on the side for a tangy contrast.
    - **Seaweed:** Sprinkle with seaweed strips or shredded nori for additional flavor and texture.

Notes:

- **Sushi-Grade Tuna:** Use sushi-grade tuna for the best flavor and safety. Make sure to source it from a reputable fish market or grocery store.
- **Adjust Spice Level:** Adjust the amount of Sriracha sauce to suit your spice preference. You can add more or less depending on your taste.
- **Avocado:** Adding avocado is optional but adds a creamy texture and complements the spicy tuna nicely.
- **Rice:** For the best texture, use sushi rice or short-grain rice. If you don't have access to sushi rice, any medium or short-grain rice will work.
- **Storage:** Spicy tuna should be served fresh. If you have leftovers, store the spicy tuna mixture separately from the rice and vegetables and consume it within a day.

Spicy Tuna Don is a delightful and customizable dish that offers a fresh and spicy twist on traditional rice bowls. Enjoy the rich flavors and textures in this easy and satisfying meal!

Zaru Soba (Chilled Soba Noodles)

Ingredients:

For the Soba Noodles:

- 8 oz (225g) soba noodles (buckwheat noodles)
- Water (for boiling)
- Ice (for cooling)

For the Dipping Sauce (Tsuyu):

- 1/2 cup soy sauce
- 1/4 cup mirin (sweet rice wine)
- 1/4 cup dashi stock (or use water if dashi is not available)
- 1 tablespoon sugar (optional)

For Garnishing:

- 2-3 green onions, finely sliced
- 1 tablespoon sesame seeds, toasted
- 1/2 cup grated daikon radish (optional)
- 1 sheet nori (seaweed), cut into thin strips (optional)
- Wasabi (optional)

Instructions:

1. **Prepare the Dipping Sauce (Tsuyu):**
   - **Combine Ingredients:** In a small saucepan, combine soy sauce, mirin, and dashi stock. If you like, add 1 tablespoon of sugar to balance the flavor.
   - **Heat:** Bring the mixture to a simmer over medium heat, stirring occasionally. Once the sugar is dissolved, remove from heat and let cool. You can chill it in the refrigerator until ready to use.
2. **Cook the Soba Noodles:**
   - **Boil Water:** Bring a large pot of water to a boil.
   - **Cook Noodles:** Add the soba noodles and cook according to the package instructions, usually for about 4-5 minutes. Stir occasionally to prevent sticking.
   - **Cool Noodles:** Once cooked, drain the noodles in a colander and rinse them under cold running water to stop the cooking process and remove excess starch. Transfer the noodles to a bowl filled with ice water to cool them completely.
3. **Prepare Garnishes:**
   - **Slice Green Onions:** Finely slice the green onions.
   - **Toast Sesame Seeds:** Toast sesame seeds in a dry skillet over medium heat until golden brown and fragrant.
   - **Grate Daikon:** If using, grate the daikon radish.
   - **Cut Nori:** Cut the nori into thin strips.
4. **Assemble and Serve:**

- **Drain Noodles:** Once the noodles are chilled, drain them well and arrange them on a serving plate or bamboo mat (zaru).
- **Serve:** Place the dipping sauce (tsuyu) in small bowls for dipping. Serve the noodles with the garnishes on the side. Each person can dip the noodles into the sauce and enjoy with the toppings of their choice.

Notes:

- **Soba Noodles:** Soba noodles are made from buckwheat flour and have a distinctive flavor and texture. They can be found in Asian grocery stores or supermarkets.
- **Dashi Stock:** Dashi is a traditional Japanese stock made from kombu (seaweed) and bonito flakes (dried fish). You can use instant dashi powder or granules if you don't have homemade dashi.
- **Serving Temperature:** Zaru soba is typically served cold, but if you prefer, you can serve the dipping sauce warm.
- **Garnishes:** The garnishes add different textures and flavors. Adjust them according to your taste preferences. Wasabi can be added to the dipping sauce for a spicy kick.

Zaru Soba is a delightful and light dish that's perfect for a quick meal or a refreshing summer treat. Its simplicity and versatility make it a staple in Japanese cuisine. Enjoy the clean, crisp flavors and the fun of dipping the noodles into the flavorful tsuyu sauce!

Shabu-Shabu Salad

Ingredients:

For the Shabu-Shabu:

- 8 oz (225g) thinly sliced beef (such as sirloin or ribeye, often found labeled for shabu-shabu)
- 4 cups water or beef broth (for boiling)

For the Salad:

- 4 cups mixed salad greens (such as lettuce, arugula, or spinach)
- 1 cucumber, thinly sliced
- 1/2 red bell pepper, thinly sliced
- 1 small carrot, julienned
- 1/4 cup cherry tomatoes, halved
- 1/4 cup radishes, thinly sliced (optional)
- 1/4 cup edamame (optional, cooked and shelled)

For the Dressing:

- 1/4 cup soy sauce
- 2 tablespoons rice vinegar
- 1 tablespoon sesame oil
- 1 tablespoon sugar or honey
- 1 teaspoon grated fresh ginger
- 1 clove garlic, minced
- 1 tablespoon sesame seeds (optional)
- 1 tablespoon chopped fresh cilantro or parsley (optional)

For Garnishing:

- Pickled ginger (optional)
- Sliced green onions
- Additional sesame seeds

Instructions:

1. **Prepare the Shabu-Shabu:**
    - **Boil Water:** In a pot, bring 4 cups of water or beef broth to a boil.
    - **Cook Beef:** Add the thinly sliced beef to the boiling liquid, cooking for just 20-30 seconds until the beef is no longer pink. Do not overcook.
    - **Cool Beef:** Using a slotted spoon, transfer the cooked beef to a bowl of ice water to cool. Once cool, drain and pat the beef dry with paper towels.
2. **Prepare the Salad:**
    - **Chop Vegetables:** Prepare the salad ingredients by slicing and julienning the vegetables as needed. Arrange them on a large salad plate or bowl.

- **Add Shabu-Shabu Beef:** Slice the cooled beef into bite-sized pieces and add it to the salad.
3. **Make the Dressing:**
    - **Combine Ingredients:** In a small bowl, whisk together soy sauce, rice vinegar, sesame oil, sugar or honey, grated ginger, and minced garlic. Taste and adjust the seasoning if needed.
    - **Add Garnishes:** Optionally, stir in sesame seeds and chopped cilantro or parsley.
4. **Assemble and Serve:**
    - **Dress the Salad:** Drizzle the dressing over the salad just before serving.
    - **Garnish:** Garnish with pickled ginger, sliced green onions, and additional sesame seeds if desired.

Notes:

- **Beef:** The key to shabu-shabu is using thinly sliced beef, which cooks very quickly. If you can't find pre-sliced beef, partially freeze a piece of beef to make it easier to slice thinly.
- **Broth:** If using water, you may want to season it lightly with salt or soy sauce to add flavor to the beef as it cooks.
- **Vegetable Variations:** Feel free to add other vegetables such as bell peppers, snap peas, or baby corn based on your preferences and seasonal availability.
- **Dressing:** Adjust the sweetness and acidity of the dressing to your taste. You can add more sugar or vinegar if needed.

Shabu-Shabu Salad is a versatile and light dish that's perfect for showcasing the flavors of Japanese cuisine in a fresh and vibrant way. Enjoy the balance of tender beef, crisp vegetables, and zesty dressing in this delightful salad!

Japanese Cheesecake

Ingredients:

For the Cheesecake:

- 8 oz (225g) cream cheese, softened
- 1/2 cup (120ml) milk
- 1/4 cup (50g) granulated sugar (for cream cheese mixture)
- 1/4 cup (50g) granulated sugar (for egg whites)
- 4 large eggs, separated
- 1/4 cup (30g) all-purpose flour
- 1 tablespoon cornstarch
- 1/2 teaspoon vanilla extract
- 1/2 teaspoon lemon juice (optional, for added flavor)
- 1/4 teaspoon cream of tartar (optional, to stabilize egg whites)

For the Water Bath:

- Boiling water (enough to reach halfway up the sides of the cake pan)

Instructions:

1. **Prepare the Cake Pan:**
   - **Preheat Oven:** Preheat your oven to 325°F (160°C).
   - **Line Pan:** Line the bottom of an 8-inch (20cm) round springform pan with parchment paper. Grease the sides of the pan with butter or non-stick spray.
2. **Make the Cream Cheese Mixture:**
   - **Combine Ingredients:** In a heatproof bowl, combine the cream cheese and milk. Place the bowl over a pot of simmering water (double boiler method) and heat gently, stirring occasionally, until the cream cheese is melted and smooth.
   - **Add Sugar and Flour:** Remove from heat and mix in 1/4 cup of sugar. Gradually sift in the flour and cornstarch, whisking until smooth. Stir in the egg yolks, one at a time, followed by the vanilla extract and lemon juice (if using). Set aside.
3. **Prepare the Egg Whites:**
   - **Beat Egg Whites:** In a clean, dry bowl, beat the egg whites with an electric mixer until frothy. If using, add the cream of tartar to stabilize the egg whites.
   - **Add Sugar:** Gradually add the remaining 1/4 cup of sugar while continuing to beat until stiff peaks form. The egg whites should be glossy and hold their shape.
4. **Combine Mixtures:**
   - **Fold Together:** Gently fold one-third of the beaten egg whites into the cream cheese mixture to lighten it. Carefully fold in the remaining egg whites in two additions, being cautious not to deflate the mixture. The batter should be light and airy.
5. **Bake the Cheesecake:**
   - **Transfer Batter:** Pour the batter into the prepared springform pan.

- **Create Water Bath:** Place the springform pan into a larger baking dish or roasting pan. Carefully pour boiling water into the larger pan until it reaches halfway up the sides of the springform pan.
- **Bake:** Bake in the preheated oven for 55-65 minutes, or until the cake is set and the top is golden brown. The center should be slightly jiggly but not liquid.
- **Cool:** Turn off the oven and let the cheesecake cool in the oven with the door slightly ajar for 1 hour. This helps prevent cracking.

6. **Unmold and Serve:**
    - **Remove from Pan:** Once completely cooled, remove the cheesecake from the springform pan. Gently peel off the parchment paper.
    - **Chill:** Refrigerate for at least 4 hours or overnight before serving to allow the cheesecake to set fully.

Notes:

- **Egg Whites:** Ensure that your mixing bowl and beaters are completely clean and free of any fat or grease, as this can prevent the egg whites from whipping properly.
- **Flour and Cornstarch:** These ingredients help stabilize the cake and give it a fluffy texture. Do not skip or substitute them.
- **Water Bath:** The water bath helps to evenly cook the cheesecake and prevents cracking. Make sure the water is boiling when added.
- **Serving:** Japanese cheesecake can be enjoyed plain or with a dusting of powdered sugar. It can also be served with fresh fruit, whipped cream, or a light fruit glaze if desired.

Japanese Cheesecake is a delightful treat with a unique texture that sets it apart from other cheesecakes. Its light and airy consistency makes it a perfect dessert for any occasion. Enjoy the fluffy, delicate flavors of this classic Japanese dessert!

Matcha Tiramisu

Ingredients:

For the Matcha Mixture:

- 2 tablespoons matcha green tea powder (high-quality)
- 1/4 cup hot water

For the Mascarpone Cream:

- 8 oz (225g) mascarpone cheese, softened
- 1/2 cup heavy cream
- 1/2 cup granulated sugar
- 1 teaspoon vanilla extract

For the Ladyfingers:

- 24-30 ladyfingers (savoiardi)
- 1/2 cup hot water
- 2 tablespoons sugar (optional, for sweetening the soaking liquid)
- 2 tablespoons matcha green tea powder

For Garnishing:

- Extra matcha powder for dusting
- Fresh berries (optional)
- Sweetened red bean paste (optional)

Instructions:

1. **Prepare the Matcha Mixture:**
    - **Mix Matcha:** In a small bowl, whisk together the matcha powder and hot water until smooth and dissolved. Let it cool to room temperature.
2. **Prepare the Mascarpone Cream:**
    - **Whip Cream:** In a medium bowl, whip the heavy cream until soft peaks form.
    - **Combine Mascarpone:** In another bowl, whisk together the mascarpone cheese, granulated sugar, and vanilla extract until smooth.
    - **Fold Together:** Gently fold the whipped cream into the mascarpone mixture until well combined. Be careful not to deflate the mixture.
3. **Prepare the Ladyfingers:**
    - **Make Soaking Liquid:** In a shallow dish, mix together the hot water, matcha powder, and optional sugar until the matcha is fully dissolved.
    - **Soak Ladyfingers:** Briefly dip each ladyfinger into the matcha mixture, making sure not to soak them too long (they should be moist but not soggy). Arrange the soaked ladyfingers in a single layer at the bottom of your serving dish.

4. **Assemble the Tiramisu:**
   - **Layer:** Spread half of the mascarpone cream over the layer of soaked ladyfingers.
   - **Add Another Layer:** Add another layer of soaked ladyfingers on top of the cream, then spread the remaining mascarpone cream evenly over the top.
5. **Chill and Serve:**
   - **Refrigerate:** Cover and refrigerate the tiramisu for at least 4 hours, or preferably overnight, to allow the flavors to meld and the dessert to set.
   - **Garnish:** Just before serving, dust the top of the tiramisu with extra matcha powder. You can also add fresh berries or a small dollop of sweetened red bean paste for extra flavor and decoration.

Notes:

- **Matcha Quality:** Use high-quality matcha powder for the best flavor and color. Culinary grade matcha can be used for the soaking liquid, but ceremonial grade is preferred for the mascarpone cream.
- **Ladyfingers:** Store-bought ladyfingers work well, but you can also make your own if you prefer. They should be firm enough to hold their shape when dipped in liquid.
- **Serving Dish:** This recipe can be made in a large dish or individual serving cups. Adjust the layers accordingly.
- **Texture:** The key to a successful tiramisu is to achieve a good balance of moistness and creaminess. Avoid over-soaking the ladyfingers, as they should be soft but not mushy.

Matcha Tiramisu offers a unique and delightful fusion of Italian and Japanese flavors, perfect for a sophisticated dessert or a special occasion. Enjoy the creamy, matcha-infused layers and the subtle green tea taste in this elegant treat!

Mochi Ice Cream

Ingredients:

For the Mochi Dough:

- 1 cup mochiko (sweet rice flour, also known as glutinous rice flour)
- 1/2 cup granulated sugar
- 1 cup water
- 1 tablespoon cornstarch (for dusting)

For the Ice Cream:

- 1 pint (2 cups) of your favorite ice cream (softened for easier scooping)

For Garnishing (Optional):

- Additional cornstarch or powdered sugar (for dusting)
- Fresh fruit or chocolate sauce (optional, for serving)

Instructions:

1. **Prepare the Mochi Dough:**
    - **Mix Ingredients:** In a heatproof bowl, combine mochiko and sugar. Gradually add water, mixing until smooth.
    - **Steam:** Cover the bowl with plastic wrap or a lid and steam the mixture for about 20-25 minutes, or until it becomes translucent and slightly sticky. Stir halfway through steaming.
    - **Cool:** Allow the mochi dough to cool slightly, but keep it warm enough to handle.
2. **Prepare the Ice Cream:**
    - **Soften Ice Cream:** Let the ice cream sit at room temperature for about 10-15 minutes, or until it is soft enough to scoop easily.
3. **Shape the Mochi Ice Cream:**
    - **Dust Surface:** Lightly dust a clean surface with cornstarch or powdered sugar to prevent sticking.
    - **Divide Mochi Dough:** Turn the mochi dough out onto the dusted surface and divide it into small pieces (about 1.5-2 inch squares).
    - **Flatten Dough:** Using a rolling pin or your hands, flatten each piece of dough into a thin round, about 1/8 inch thick.
    - **Scoop Ice Cream:** Scoop a small amount of softened ice cream (about 1 tablespoon) onto the center of each mochi round.
    - **Wrap and Seal:** Gently fold the edges of the mochi dough around the ice cream, pinching to seal. Be careful not to tear the mochi dough.
4. **Freeze:**
    - **Freeze Mochi Ice Cream:** Place the wrapped mochi ice cream balls on a parchment-lined tray. Freeze for at least 2 hours, or until the ice cream is firm.

5. **Serve:**
   - **Serve:** Remove from the freezer just before serving. Dust with additional cornstarch or powdered sugar if needed to prevent sticking.

Notes:

- **Flavors:** You can use any flavor of ice cream you like, such as vanilla, chocolate, strawberry, or matcha. For a more traditional flavor, try using red bean paste or green tea ice cream.
- **Mochiko:** Mochiko (sweet rice flour) is different from regular rice flour and is essential for the proper texture of mochi.
- **Handling:** Mochi dough can be sticky, so keep your hands and work surface dusted with cornstarch to make handling easier.
- **Storage:** Mochi ice cream can be stored in the freezer for up to a month. Make sure to keep them well-sealed to avoid freezer burn.

Mochi Ice Cream offers a delightful combination of creamy ice cream and chewy mochi, making it a fun and refreshing dessert. Enjoy experimenting with different flavors and fillings to find your perfect mochi ice cream combination!

Kakigori (Shaved Ice)

Ingredients:

For the Shaved Ice:

- 2 cups ice cubes (or use a block of ice if you have an ice shaver)

For the Syrups and Toppings (Customize to Your Preference):

- **Matcha Syrup:** 1/2 cup sugar, 1/4 cup water, 1 tablespoon matcha green tea powder
- **Strawberry Syrup:** 1 cup fresh strawberries, 1/2 cup sugar, 1/4 cup water
- **Condensed Milk:** 1/2 cup sweetened condensed milk
- **Fruit Toppings:** Fresh fruit (e.g., strawberries, mango, kiwi), red bean paste, or mochi pieces
- **Additional Toppings:** Sweetened red bean paste, black sesame seeds, or a drizzle of syrup

Instructions:

1. **Prepare the Shaved Ice:**
   - **Shave the Ice:** If using ice cubes, use an ice shaver or blender to shave the ice into a fluffy, fine texture. If using a block of ice, an ice shaver is ideal for achieving the right consistency.
2. **Make the Syrups:**
   Matcha Syrup:
   - **Combine Ingredients:** In a small saucepan, combine sugar and water. Heat over medium heat until the sugar is completely dissolved.
   - **Add Matcha:** Remove from heat and whisk in the matcha powder until fully dissolved. Let it cool.
3. **Strawberry Syrup:**
   - **Cook Strawberries:** In a saucepan, combine strawberries, sugar, and water. Cook over medium heat, stirring occasionally, until the strawberries break down and the mixture thickens (about 10 minutes).
   - **Blend and Strain:** Use an immersion blender to puree the mixture until smooth. Strain through a fine mesh sieve to remove seeds. Let it cool.
4. **Assemble the Kakigori:**
   - **Scoop Shaved Ice:** Place a generous amount of shaved ice into serving bowls.
   - **Add Syrups:** Drizzle your choice of syrups (such as matcha or strawberry) over the shaved ice. You can layer different syrups or combine them for a unique flavor.
   - **Add Toppings:** Add fresh fruit, mochi pieces, sweetened red bean paste, or other toppings as desired.
   - **Finish with Condensed Milk:** Drizzle sweetened condensed milk over the top for extra sweetness and creaminess.

5. **Serve:**
   - **Enjoy Immediately:** Serve immediately after assembling to enjoy the refreshing texture of the shaved ice.

Notes:

- **Texture:** The texture of kakigori is key; aim for very fine, fluffy ice. If using a blender, pulse the ice cubes gently to avoid making the ice too granular.
- **Flavor Combinations:** Feel free to experiment with different syrups and toppings to create your own variations of kakigori. Other popular syrups include caramel, chocolate, or fruit-based syrups.
- **Mochi:** For an authentic touch, you can add small pieces of mochi to the top of the shaved ice.

Kakigori is a versatile and customizable dessert, perfect for cooling down on a hot day or enjoying as a sweet treat. Its light, refreshing nature makes it a favorite summer dessert in Japan and beyond. Enjoy creating your own variations with your favorite flavors and toppings!

Red Bean Soup (Zenzai)

Ingredients:

For the Soup:

- 1 cup dried azuki beans (or 2 cups canned azuki beans)
- 4 cups water (for cooking dried beans)
- 1/2 cup granulated sugar (adjust to taste)
- 1/4 teaspoon salt
- 1 tablespoon soy sauce (optional, for depth of flavor)

For Serving (Optional):

- Mochi (sweet rice cakes)
- Sweetened condensed milk (optional)
- Shaved ice (for cold zenzai)
- Fresh fruit (e.g., strawberries, oranges, or a light fruit syrup)

Instructions:

1. **Prepare the Azuki Beans:**
   - **If Using Dried Beans:** Rinse the dried azuki beans under cold water. Place them in a large pot with 4 cups of water. Bring to a boil, then reduce the heat and simmer for 5 minutes. Drain and rinse the beans, then return them to the pot with fresh water (about 4 cups). Bring to a boil again, then simmer for 1-1.5 hours, or until the beans are soft. Keep an eye on the water level and add more if necessary.
   - **If Using Canned Beans:** Simply drain and rinse the canned beans.
2. **Make the Soup:**
   - **Cook Beans:** If using dried beans, after cooking and softening them, drain any excess water and return the beans to the pot. Add 4 cups of fresh water to the beans. Simmer for 10 minutes to allow the flavors to meld.
   - **Sweeten:** Stir in the granulated sugar and salt. Continue to cook for an additional 5-10 minutes until the beans are fully tender and the soup has thickened slightly.
   - **Optional Soy Sauce:** For added depth of flavor, stir in 1 tablespoon of soy sauce if desired. Adjust the sweetness if needed.
3. **Prepare Accompaniments (Optional):**
   - **Cook Mochi:** If serving with mochi, grill or toast the mochi until lightly browned and puffy. You can also pan-fry or microwave the mochi, depending on your preference.
   - **Prepare Other Toppings:** Prepare any additional toppings like sweetened condensed milk or fresh fruit.
4. **Serve:**

- **Hot:** Ladle the red bean soup into bowls and serve hot with pieces of mochi if desired.
- **Cold:** For a refreshing summer treat, allow the soup to cool, then chill in the refrigerator. Serve cold over shaved ice or with a dollop of sweetened condensed milk.

Notes:

- **Sweetness:** Adjust the amount of sugar to your taste. Some prefer their zenzai sweeter or less sweet, so feel free to modify the sugar amount as needed.
- **Texture:** Traditional zenzai can vary in texture from a chunky bean mixture to a smoother, more soup-like consistency. Adjust the thickness by adding more water or mashing some of the beans to achieve your desired texture.
- **Mochi:** Mochi is a classic accompaniment, but you can also enjoy zenzai with other treats or plain. The soft, chewy texture of mochi pairs well with the sweet, creamy beans.
- **Storage:** Zenzai can be stored in the refrigerator for up to a week. If storing, reheat gently on the stove or in the microwave before serving.

Red Bean Soup (Zenzai) is a comforting and versatile dessert that highlights the natural sweetness and rich flavor of azuki beans. Whether enjoyed hot or cold, it's a delightful way to experience a traditional Japanese treat.

Japanese Pumpkin Tempura

Ingredients:

For the Tempura Batter:

- 1 cup all-purpose flour
- 1/4 cup cornstarch
- 1 large egg, lightly beaten
- 1 cup cold sparkling water (or very cold water)
- 1/4 teaspoon baking powder (optional, for extra crispiness)
- Pinch of salt

For the Pumpkin:

- 1 small Japanese pumpkin (kabocha), sliced into thin wedges (about 1/4 inch thick)
- 1/4 cup all-purpose flour (for dusting)

For Frying:

- Vegetable oil (for deep frying)

For Serving (Optional):

- Tempura dipping sauce (tentsuyu)
- Grated daikon radish
- Lemon wedges
- Sea salt or flavored salt

Instructions:

1. **Prepare the Pumpkin:**
    - **Slice Pumpkin:** Cut the kabocha pumpkin in half and remove the seeds. Slice the pumpkin into thin wedges or rounds (about 1/4 inch thick). Leave the skin on for added texture and flavor.
    - **Dust with Flour:** Lightly coat the pumpkin slices with flour. This helps the batter adhere better.
2. **Make the Tempura Batter:**
    - **Combine Dry Ingredients:** In a bowl, mix together the flour, cornstarch, and baking powder (if using).
    - **Add Wet Ingredients:** Add the beaten egg and cold sparkling water to the dry ingredients. Gently mix until just combined. The batter should be lumpy; do not overmix. The sparkling water helps create a light and crispy texture.
3. **Heat the Oil:**

- **Prepare Oil:** In a deep pan or fryer, heat enough vegetable oil to submerge the pumpkin slices. Heat the oil to about 350°F (175°C).
4. **Fry the Pumpkin:**
    - **Coat and Fry:** Dip each pumpkin slice into the tempura batter, allowing any excess batter to drip off. Carefully lower the coated pumpkin slices into the hot oil, being careful not to overcrowd the pan.
    - **Cook Until Crispy:** Fry the pumpkin slices for about 2-3 minutes, or until they are golden brown and crispy. Turn them occasionally for even cooking.
    - **Drain:** Remove the fried pumpkin slices from the oil with a slotted spoon and drain on paper towels to remove excess oil.
5. **Serve:**
    - **Arrange:** Serve the tempura hot with dipping sauce (tentsuyu) and garnishes like grated daikon radish and lemon wedges. You can also sprinkle a bit of sea salt or flavored salt for extra flavor.

Notes:

- **Pumpkin Choice:** Kabocha pumpkin is preferred for its sweet flavor and creamy texture, but you can also use other types of squash or pumpkin if kabocha is not available.
- **Batter:** The batter should be cold and slightly lumpy to achieve the best texture. The cold sparkling water or ice-cold water helps create a crispy coating.
- **Frying:** Maintain the oil temperature to ensure the tempura cooks evenly and stays crispy. If the oil temperature drops too low, the tempura may become greasy.
- **Dipping Sauce:** Tentsuyu, a tempura dipping sauce, is typically served with tempura. It is made from a mixture of dashi, soy sauce, and mirin. You can also serve tempura with a simple soy sauce or ponzu sauce.

Japanese Pumpkin Tempura is a delightful appetizer or side dish that combines the sweet, nutty flavor of kabocha pumpkin with a light, crispy batter. It's perfect for enjoying as part of a Japanese meal or as a tasty snack.

Yakitori (Grilled Chicken Skewers)

Ingredients:

For the Yakitori:

- 1 lb (450 g) chicken thighs, boneless and skinless
- 1 red bell pepper, cut into chunks
- 1 small onion, cut into chunks
- 1 zucchini, sliced into rounds
- 1 bunch of green onions, cut into 2-inch pieces

For the Tare (Yakitori Sauce):

- 1/2 cup soy sauce
- 1/2 cup mirin
- 1/4 cup sake
- 1/4 cup granulated sugar
- 1 tablespoon cornstarch mixed with 1 tablespoon water (optional, for thickening)

For the Salt Version (Shio Yakitori):

- Coarse sea salt (to taste)

For Garnishing (Optional):

- Sesame seeds
- Chopped green onions
- Lemon wedges

For Skewers:

- Bamboo skewers, soaked in water for 30 minutes

Instructions:

1. **Prepare the Chicken:**
   - **Cut Chicken:** Cut the chicken thighs into bite-sized pieces (about 1-inch cubes). You can also use chicken breast if you prefer, but thighs are more traditional for their tenderness and flavor.
2. **Prepare the Vegetables:**
   - **Cut Vegetables:** Cut the bell pepper, onion, zucchini, and green onions into pieces that will fit well on the skewers.
3. **Make the Tare Sauce (Optional):**

- **Combine Ingredients:** In a small saucepan, combine soy sauce, mirin, sake, and sugar. Bring to a boil over medium heat, stirring until the sugar dissolves.
- **Simmer:** Reduce the heat and let it simmer for 5-10 minutes until slightly thickened. If you prefer a thicker sauce, mix cornstarch with water and stir it into the sauce. Cook for an additional minute until thickened.
- **Cool:** Allow the sauce to cool. It can be stored in the refrigerator for up to a week.

4. **Skewer the Ingredients:**
   - **Assemble Skewers:** Thread the chicken pieces and vegetables onto the soaked bamboo skewers, alternating as you like. You can make skewers with just chicken or include a mix of vegetables.
5. **Grill the Yakitori:**
   - **Preheat Grill:** Preheat your grill to medium-high heat. If using a charcoal grill, allow the coals to reach a steady temperature.
   - **Grill:** Place the skewers on the grill. Grill the chicken for about 2-3 minutes on each side, or until cooked through and slightly charred. Brush with tare sauce during the last few minutes of grilling for added flavor. If making shio yakitori, sprinkle the chicken with sea salt before grilling.
   - **Turn Occasionally:** Turn the skewers occasionally to ensure even cooking and avoid burning.
6. **Serve:**
   - **Garnish:** Remove the skewers from the grill and transfer to a serving plate. Garnish with sesame seeds, chopped green onions, and lemon wedges if desired.
   - **Enjoy:** Serve immediately, either with extra tare sauce on the side or just as is.

Notes:

- **Chicken Cuts:** Chicken thighs are preferred for their rich flavor and moisture, but chicken breast can be used if desired.
- **Skewer Soaking:** Soaking bamboo skewers prevents them from burning during grilling.
- **Grilling Tips:** Keep an eye on the grill to prevent burning. If using a stovetop grill pan, cook over medium-high heat and watch closely.
- **Vegetable Options:** Feel free to add other vegetables like mushrooms, cherry tomatoes, or bell peppers to your skewers.

Yakitori is a versatile and flavorful dish that's perfect for casual gatherings or weeknight dinners. Enjoy the smoky, savory taste of grilled chicken with a touch of sweetness and umami from the tare sauce or simply seasoned with sea salt.

Shirasu (Whitebait) Rice Bowl

Ingredients:

For the Rice Bowl:

- 2 cups steamed white rice (or short-grain rice)
- 1 cup shirasu (whitebait), either fresh or preserved
- 1 tablespoon soy sauce
- 1 teaspoon mirin
- 1 tablespoon sesame seeds (optional)
- 1 teaspoon seaweed flakes (nori), cut into strips or crumbled
- 1-2 scallions (green onions), finely chopped

For Garnishing (Optional):

- Pickled vegetables (tsukemono)
- Soft-boiled egg or raw egg yolk
- Shredded daikon radish
- Fresh herbs (e.g., shiso leaves or parsley)

Instructions:

1. **Prepare the Rice:**
    - **Cook Rice:** Cook the rice according to the package instructions or using a rice cooker. It should be warm when assembling the rice bowl.
2. **Prepare the Shirasu:**
    - **Season Shirasu:** If using fresh shirasu, lightly rinse them under cold water and pat dry. If using preserved shirasu (often found in jars), they are ready to use as-is.
    - **Optional Seasoning:** Toss the shirasu with soy sauce and mirin for added flavor. If the shirasu is already seasoned, this step may not be necessary.
3. **Assemble the Rice Bowl:**
    - **Layer Rice:** Scoop the warm rice into individual serving bowls.
    - **Add Shirasu:** Place a generous amount of shirasu over the top of the rice.
4. **Garnish:**
    - **Add Toppings:** Sprinkle with sesame seeds, seaweed flakes, and chopped scallions.
    - **Additional Garnishes:** Add any additional garnishes like pickled vegetables, a soft-boiled egg, or shredded daikon radish.
5. **Serve:**
    - **Enjoy:** Serve immediately while the rice is still warm.

Notes:

- **Shirasu Availability:** Shirasu can be found at Asian grocery stores or Japanese markets. If you can't find shirasu, you can substitute with other small fish like anchovies or sardines, though the flavor and texture may differ slightly.
- **Rice Type:** Short-grain rice is typically used in Japanese dishes for its sticky texture, but you can use other types of rice if preferred.
- **Seasoning:** If the shirasu is already salty or flavored, adjust the amount of additional soy sauce or salt accordingly.
- **Egg Option:** Adding a raw egg yolk on top of the rice bowl is a common practice in Japan, providing a rich, creamy texture. Ensure the egg is from a reputable source if consuming raw.

Shirasu Rice Bowl is a comforting and nutritious meal, showcasing the delicate flavor of shirasu with minimal fuss. It's a great way to enjoy the simplicity and freshness of Japanese cuisine.

Mentaiko Pasta

Ingredients:

For the Pasta:

- 8 oz (225 g) spaghetti or other pasta of choice
- 1 tablespoon salt (for pasta water)
- 1 tablespoon olive oil

For the Sauce:

- 1/2 cup mentaiko (cod roe), removed from the membrane
- 2 tablespoons unsalted butter
- 1/4 cup heavy cream
- 2 tablespoons soy sauce
- 1 tablespoon sake (or white wine)
- 1 clove garlic, minced
- 1 tablespoon chopped fresh parsley (optional, for garnish)
- 1 tablespoon nori (seaweed) strips or flakes (optional, for garnish)
- 1 tablespoon toasted sesame seeds (optional, for garnish)

Instructions:

1. **Cook the Pasta:**
   - **Boil Water:** Bring a large pot of salted water to a boil.
   - **Cook Pasta:** Add the spaghetti and cook according to the package instructions until al dente. Reserve about 1/2 cup of pasta water, then drain the pasta and return it to the pot.
2. **Prepare the Sauce:**
   - **Melt Butter:** In a large skillet, heat the butter over medium heat until melted.
   - **Sauté Garlic:** Add the minced garlic and cook for about 1 minute, until fragrant but not browned.
   - **Add Mentaiko:** Reduce heat to low and add the mentaiko to the skillet. Cook gently, stirring frequently, for about 2-3 minutes. Mentaiko cooks quickly, so avoid high heat to prevent it from becoming too dry.
   - **Add Cream and Seasonings:** Stir in the heavy cream, soy sauce, and sake. Cook for another 1-2 minutes, allowing the sauce to combine and thicken slightly.
3. **Combine Pasta and Sauce:**
   - **Mix Pasta and Sauce:** Add the cooked pasta to the skillet with the sauce. Toss to coat the pasta evenly with the sauce. If the sauce seems too thick, add a bit of the reserved pasta water, a tablespoon at a time, until you reach the desired consistency.
4. **Garnish and Serve:**

- **Garnish:** Transfer the pasta to serving plates. Garnish with chopped parsley, nori strips, and toasted sesame seeds if desired.
- **Serve:** Serve immediately while hot.

Notes:

- **Mentaiko:** Mentaiko can be found at Japanese grocery stores or Asian markets. If fresh mentaiko is unavailable, you can use mentaiko paste or roe from a jar.
- **Creaminess:** Adjust the amount of heavy cream based on your preference for sauce thickness. You can also add a bit more butter for extra richness.
- **Spice Level:** Mentaiko can vary in spiciness. Taste the roe before adding it to the sauce and adjust the amount or add a bit of chili flakes if you prefer more heat.
- **Alternative Add-ins:** You can add other ingredients like sautéed mushrooms, scallions, or cooked shrimp for additional flavor and texture.

Mentaiko Pasta is a fusion dish that highlights the rich, briny flavor of cod roe, creating a deliciously creamy and satisfying pasta. It's a great example of how Japanese ingredients can be used to elevate classic Italian dishes.

Takoyaki Okonomiyaki

Ingredients:

For the Takoyaki Balls:

- 1 cup takoyaki batter (store-bought or homemade)
- 1/2 cup cooked octopus, diced (or substitute with shrimp or a mix of vegetables)
- 2 tablespoons pickled ginger, finely chopped
- 2 tablespoons green onions, chopped
- 1 tablespoon tempura scraps (tenkasu) or crushed rice crackers
- 1/2 cup shredded mozzarella cheese (optional, for extra richness)

For the Okonomiyaki Batter:

- 1 cup all-purpose flour
- 1/2 cup dashi broth (or water)
- 1 large egg
- 1/2 cup shredded cabbage
- 1/4 cup grated carrots
- 1/4 cup chopped green onions
- 1/4 cup cooked bacon or pork belly, diced (optional)
- 1 tablespoon soy sauce
- 1 teaspoon baking powder
- 1/2 teaspoon salt

For Toppings:

- Okonomiyaki sauce
- Japanese mayonnaise
- Aonori (dried seaweed flakes)
- Katsuobushi (bonito flakes)
- Pickled ginger (beni shoga)
- Green onions, sliced

Instructions:

1. **Prepare Takoyaki Balls:**
    - **Make Takoyaki Batter:** Follow the instructions on your takoyaki batter mix or make your own batter using flour, dashi, and egg.
    - **Preheat Takoyaki Pan:** Heat a takoyaki pan over medium heat and lightly oil the molds.

- **Add Ingredients:** Pour the takoyaki batter into each mold, filling it halfway. Add a few pieces of octopus, pickled ginger, green onions, and tempura scraps to each mold. Top with a small amount of shredded cheese if using.
- **Cook Takoyaki:** Cook the takoyaki for 2-3 minutes, turning them with a skewer or chopsticks until they are golden brown and crispy on the outside. Remove and set aside.

2. **Prepare Okonomiyaki Batter:**
    - **Mix Batter:** In a large bowl, combine flour, dashi broth, egg, soy sauce, baking powder, and salt. Mix until smooth.
    - **Add Vegetables:** Fold in shredded cabbage, grated carrots, chopped green onions, and diced bacon or pork belly.
3. **Cook Okonomiyaki:**
    - **Heat a Skillet:** Heat a large skillet or griddle over medium heat and lightly oil it.
    - **Cook Pancake:** Pour the okonomiyaki batter into the skillet, spreading it into a large circle about 1/2-inch thick. Cook for 3-4 minutes until the bottom is golden brown.
    - **Flip and Cook:** Carefully flip the pancake and cook the other side for another 3-4 minutes until golden brown and cooked through.
4. **Assemble Takoyaki Okonomiyaki:**
    - **Top with Takoyaki:** Place the cooked takoyaki balls on top of the okonomiyaki pancake.
    - **Add Toppings:** Drizzle okonomiyaki sauce and Japanese mayonnaise over the top. Sprinkle with aonori, katsuobushi, and extra green onions.
5. **Serve:**
    - **Enjoy:** Cut into slices and serve hot, garnished with pickled ginger and additional toppings as desired.

Notes:

- **Takoyaki Pan:** If you don't have a takoyaki pan, you can make takoyaki balls using a muffin tin or a special takoyaki mold, or you can omit them and make a plain okonomiyaki.
- **Substitutions:** Feel free to substitute octopus with other proteins or vegetables based on your preference.
- **Toppings:** Adjust the amount of okonomiyaki sauce and mayonnaise to taste. You can also add other toppings like bonito flakes and nori for extra flavor.

Takoyaki Okonomiyaki is a fun and flavorful fusion dish that brings together the best of both takoyaki and okonomiyaki. It's perfect for sharing with friends and family or for a special treat when you're craving something a bit different.

Sukiyaki Beef Rolls

Ingredients:

For the Beef Rolls:

- 1 lb (450 g) thinly sliced beef (such as ribeye or sirloin)
- 1 small carrot, cut into thin matchsticks
- 1 cup shiitake mushrooms, sliced
- 1/2 cup asparagus, cut into 2-inch pieces
- 1/2 cup Japanese leeks or green onions, cut into 2-inch pieces
- 2 tablespoons vegetable oil

For the Sukiyaki Sauce:

- 1/2 cup soy sauce
- 1/4 cup mirin
- 1/4 cup sake
- 3 tablespoons sugar
- 1 cup dashi broth (or water)

For Garnishing (Optional):

- Shredded nori (seaweed)
- Sesame seeds
- Chopped green onions
- Pickled ginger

Instructions:

1. **Prepare the Vegetables:**
   - **Cut Vegetables:** Cut the carrots into thin matchsticks, slice the shiitake mushrooms, and cut the asparagus and green onions into 2-inch pieces.
2. **Prepare the Beef:**
   - **Season Beef:** Lay out the thinly sliced beef on a clean surface. You can season with a small pinch of salt and pepper if desired.
   - **Roll Filling:** Place a few pieces of each vegetable onto a slice of beef. Carefully roll the beef around the vegetables, securing with toothpicks if necessary. Repeat until all the beef and vegetables are used.
3. **Make the Sukiyaki Sauce:**
   - **Combine Ingredients:** In a bowl, mix together the soy sauce, mirin, sake, sugar, and dashi broth. Stir until the sugar is dissolved.
4. **Cook the Beef Rolls:**
   - **Heat Oil:** In a large skillet or frying pan, heat vegetable oil over medium heat.

- **Brown Rolls:** Add the beef rolls to the skillet and cook for 2-3 minutes on each side until the beef is browned and slightly crispy.
- **Add Sauce:** Pour the sukiyaki sauce over the beef rolls in the skillet. Bring to a simmer and cook for an additional 5-7 minutes, or until the beef is cooked through and the vegetables are tender. The sauce should thicken slightly.

5. **Serve:**
   - **Remove Toothpicks:** If you used toothpicks, carefully remove them before serving.
   - **Garnish:** Transfer the beef rolls to a serving platter. Garnish with shredded nori, sesame seeds, chopped green onions, and pickled ginger if desired.

Notes:

- **Beef Slices:** Thinly sliced beef is essential for this dish. If you cannot find pre-sliced beef, you can freeze a block of beef for 30 minutes to make slicing easier.
- **Vegetable Choices:** Feel free to add other vegetables like bell peppers, spinach, or mushrooms based on your preference.
- **Sauce Consistency:** If the sauce is too thin, let it simmer for a few extra minutes to reduce and thicken. If it's too thick, add a bit more dashi or water to adjust.
- **Serving:** Sukiyaki beef rolls can be served with steamed rice or as part of a larger Japanese meal.

Sukiyaki Beef Rolls offer a flavorful and visually appealing way to enjoy the rich tastes of sukiyaki in a more refined presentation. The combination of tender beef and crisp vegetables in a savory sauce makes this dish a standout choice for any special occasion.

Goya Champuru (Bitter Melon Stir-Fry)

Ingredients:

- 1 medium goya (bitter melon), halved and thinly sliced
- 200 g (7 oz) firm tofu, drained and cubed
- 150 g (5 oz) pork belly or thinly sliced pork (or substitute with chicken or beef)
- 1 small onion, sliced
- 1 small carrot, sliced
- 2 cloves garlic, minced
- 2 tablespoons vegetable oil
- 2 tablespoons soy sauce
- 1 tablespoon mirin
- 1 tablespoon sake (or dry white wine)
- 1/2 teaspoon sugar
- Salt and pepper to taste
- 1 tablespoon sesame seeds (optional)
- 1-2 green onions, chopped (optional, for garnish)

Instructions:

1. **Prepare the Goya:**
    - **Slice Goya:** Cut the goya in half lengthwise and scoop out the seeds. Slice thinly.
    - **Remove Bitterness (Optional):** To reduce the bitterness, you can sprinkle the sliced goya with salt and let it sit for 10 minutes. Rinse and pat dry before using.
2. **Prepare the Tofu:**
    - **Drain Tofu:** Press the tofu to remove excess moisture. Cut into cubes.
    - **Fry Tofu:** In a large skillet or wok, heat 1 tablespoon of vegetable oil over medium heat. Add the tofu cubes and fry until golden brown on all sides. Remove from the pan and set aside.
3. **Cook the Pork:**
    - **Heat Oil:** In the same skillet, add another tablespoon of vegetable oil.
    - **Cook Pork:** Add the sliced pork and cook until browned and cooked through. Remove from the pan and set aside with the tofu.
4. **Stir-Fry Vegetables:**
    - **Sauté Aromatics:** Add the sliced onion and minced garlic to the skillet. Sauté until fragrant and the onions are translucent.
    - **Add Carrots and Goya:** Add the sliced carrots and goya to the pan. Stir-fry for 5-7 minutes, until the goya is tender but still slightly crisp.
5. **Combine and Season:**
    - **Return Pork and Tofu:** Return the cooked pork and tofu to the skillet with the vegetables.

- **Add Sauce:** Stir in the soy sauce, mirin, sake, and sugar. Cook for another 2-3 minutes, stirring occasionally, until everything is well coated and heated through.
        - **Season:** Taste and adjust seasoning with salt and pepper as needed.
6. **Serve:**
    - **Garnish:** Transfer the stir-fry to a serving platter. Garnish with sesame seeds and chopped green onions if desired.

Notes:

- **Goya:** Goya (bitter melon) is a key ingredient in this dish and provides its unique flavor. If you cannot find goya, you might substitute with zucchini or another vegetable, but the taste will be different.
- **Tofu:** Firm tofu holds up well in stir-fries. You can also use silken tofu, but it will break apart more easily.
- **Pork:** Pork belly is traditional, but you can use other cuts of pork or substitute with chicken or beef based on your preference.
- **Adjusting Bitterness:** If you find goya too bitter, soaking it in salt or blanching it briefly can help reduce the bitterness.

Goya Champuru is a nutritious and hearty dish that highlights the unique flavors of Okinawan cuisine. Its combination of bitter melon with savory pork and tofu creates a satisfying meal that is both flavorful and good for you.

Tempura Soba

Ingredients:

For the Tempura:

- 8 large shrimp, peeled and deveined
- 1 medium sweet potato, peeled and sliced into thin rounds
- 1 medium zucchini, sliced into thin rounds
- 1 cup all-purpose flour
- 1 large egg
- 1 cup ice-cold water
- 1/2 teaspoon baking powder
- Vegetable oil, for frying

For the Soba Noodles:

- 8 oz (225 g) soba noodles
- 4 cups dashi broth (or water with dashi granules)
- 1/4 cup soy sauce
- 2 tablespoons mirin
- 1 tablespoon sake (or white wine)
- 1/2 teaspoon sugar

For Garnishing:

- 2 green onions, sliced
- 1 tablespoon nori (seaweed) strips
- 1 tablespoon sesame seeds
- Pickled ginger (optional)

Instructions:

1. **Prepare the Tempura Batter:**
    - **Mix Batter:** In a bowl, combine the flour, baking powder, egg, and ice-cold water. Mix gently until just combined; it's okay if there are a few lumps. Do not overmix.
    - **Prepare Ingredients:** Pat the shrimp, sweet potato, and zucchini dry with paper towels.
2. **Fry the Tempura:**
    - **Heat Oil:** In a deep pan or pot, heat vegetable oil to 350°F (175°C). You need enough oil to submerge the tempura.
    - **Coat and Fry:** Dip each piece of shrimp and vegetables into the tempura batter, allowing excess batter to drip off. Carefully place them in the hot oil. Fry in batches to avoid overcrowding. Cook until golden brown and crispy, about 2-3

minutes for shrimp and 3-4 minutes for vegetables. Remove with a slotted spoon and drain on paper towels.
3. **Prepare the Soba Noodles:**
    - **Cook Noodles:** Bring a large pot of water to a boil. Add the soba noodles and cook according to package instructions, usually 4-6 minutes. Drain and rinse under cold water to stop cooking. Set aside.
4. **Make the Broth:**
    - **Combine Ingredients:** In a saucepan, combine the dashi broth, soy sauce, mirin, sake, and sugar. Bring to a simmer over medium heat and cook for a few minutes until the sugar is dissolved. Keep warm.
5. **Assemble the Dish:**
    - **Heat Broth:** Reheat the broth if needed and divide it among serving bowls.
    - **Add Noodles:** Place a portion of soba noodles into each bowl of broth.
    - **Top with Tempura:** Arrange the tempura on top of the noodles.
    - **Garnish:** Sprinkle with sliced green onions, nori strips, and sesame seeds. Add pickled ginger if using.
6. **Serve:**
    - **Enjoy:** Serve immediately while hot.

Notes:

- **Tempura:** You can vary the tempura ingredients based on what you have available or prefer. Other common tempura items include mushrooms, bell peppers, and onions.
- **Broth:** Adjust the seasoning of the broth to taste. If you like a stronger flavor, add a bit more soy sauce or mirin.
- **Noodles:** Be sure to rinse the soba noodles after cooking to remove excess starch and prevent them from becoming sticky.

Tempura Soba is a comforting and satisfying meal that showcases the crispy and light nature of tempura alongside the hearty and flavorful soba noodles. It's perfect for a quick weeknight dinner or a special treat.

Katsu Sandwich

Ingredients:

For the Katsu:

- 2 boneless pork chops or chicken breasts (about 1/2 inch thick)
- Salt and pepper, to taste
- 1/2 cup all-purpose flour
- 1 large egg
- 1 cup panko breadcrumbs
- Vegetable oil, for frying

For the Sandwich:

- 4 slices of white bread (Japanese milk bread or any soft sandwich bread)
- 1 cup shredded cabbage
- 2 tablespoons tonkatsu sauce (or Worcestershire sauce as a substitute)
- 1 tablespoon mayonnaise
- 1 tablespoon Dijon mustard (optional)
- Pickles or Japanese-style pickled vegetables (optional)

Instructions:

1. **Prepare the Katsu:**
    - **Season Meat:** Season the pork chops or chicken breasts with salt and pepper.
    - **Dredge Meat:** Set up a breading station with three shallow dishes. Place the flour in one dish, the beaten egg in another, and the panko breadcrumbs in the third.
    - **Coat Meat:** Dredge each piece of meat in flour, shaking off excess, then dip into the beaten egg, and finally coat with panko breadcrumbs, pressing gently to adhere.
    - **Heat Oil:** Heat about 1/2 inch of vegetable oil in a large skillet over medium heat. The oil is ready when a small piece of bread dropped in sizzles immediately.
    - **Fry Katsu:** Fry the breaded cutlets for about 4-5 minutes per side, or until golden brown and cooked through. The internal temperature should reach 145°F (63°C) for pork and 165°F (74°C) for chicken. Remove from the pan and drain on paper towels.
2. **Prepare the Sandwich:**
    - **Toast Bread (Optional):** Lightly toast the bread slices if desired.
    - **Spread Condiments:** Spread mayonnaise on one side of each slice of bread. If using, spread Dijon mustard on the other side of two slices.

- **Assemble Sandwich:** Place one of the cooked katsu cutlets on top of two slices of bread. Drizzle with tonkatsu sauce. Top with shredded cabbage and, if desired, pickles or pickled vegetables.
- **Finish Sandwich:** Place the remaining slices of bread on top, mayonnaise side down.

3. **Serve:**
    - **Cut and Serve:** Cut the sandwich diagonally for easier eating. Serve immediately.

Notes:

- **Tonkatsu Sauce:** Tonkatsu sauce is a sweet and tangy sauce specifically made for tonkatsu. If you can't find it, you can use Worcestershire sauce or a mixture of ketchup and soy sauce as a substitute.
- **Bread:** For a more authentic experience, use Japanese milk bread, which is soft and slightly sweet. Regular sandwich bread works well too.
- **Cabbage:** Shredded cabbage adds crunch and freshness to the sandwich. You can also add a bit of lettuce if you like.
- **Additional Fillings:** Feel free to customize your katsu sandwich with other ingredients like sliced tomatoes or avocado.

Katsu Sandwich is a satisfying and flavorful sandwich that combines the crispy texture of the katsu with the softness of the bread and the freshness of the cabbage. It's perfect for a quick lunch or a hearty snack.

Yakimeshi (Fried Rice)

Ingredients:

- 2 cups cooked rice (preferably cold, day-old rice works best)
- 2 tablespoons vegetable oil
- 1 small onion, diced
- 2 cloves garlic, minced
- 1 cup diced cooked chicken, pork, or shrimp (or tofu for a vegetarian option)
- 1/2 cup frozen peas and carrots (or any mixed vegetables)
- 2 large eggs, lightly beaten
- 3 green onions, sliced
- 2-3 tablespoons soy sauce (to taste)
- 1 tablespoon mirin (optional)
- 1 teaspoon sesame oil
- Salt and pepper, to taste
- Pickled ginger or furikake (optional, for garnish)

Instructions:

1. **Prepare Ingredients:**
   - **Rice:** Ensure the rice is cold and separated. Freshly cooked rice can be too sticky for stir-frying.
   - **Meat/Vegetables:** Prepare and dice your meat or tofu and chop your vegetables.
2. **Cook the Base:**
   - **Heat Oil:** In a large skillet or wok, heat the vegetable oil over medium-high heat.
   - **Sauté Onion and Garlic:** Add the diced onion and minced garlic. Sauté until the onion becomes translucent and fragrant.
3. **Add Meat/Vegetables:**
   - **Cook Meat:** Add the diced meat or tofu to the skillet. Cook until heated through or slightly browned.
   - **Add Vegetables:** Stir in the frozen peas and carrots, or your choice of vegetables. Cook until they are tender and heated through.
4. **Scramble Eggs:**
   - **Push Ingredients Aside:** Push the meat and vegetables to one side of the skillet.
   - **Add Eggs:** Pour the beaten eggs into the empty side of the skillet. Scramble until cooked through, then mix with the meat and vegetables.
5. **Add Rice:**
   - **Stir-Fry Rice:** Add the cold rice to the skillet. Break up any clumps and stir-fry everything together, making sure the rice is well combined with the meat, vegetables, and eggs.
6. **Season:**

- **Add Soy Sauce and Mirin:** Drizzle soy sauce and mirin over the rice. Stir well to ensure even distribution of the seasoning.
- **Add Sesame Oil:** Drizzle sesame oil for added flavor.
- **Season to Taste:** Adjust seasoning with salt and pepper as needed.
7. **Garnish and Serve:**
    - **Add Green Onions:** Stir in the sliced green onions.
    - **Garnish:** If desired, garnish with pickled ginger or furikake.
8. **Serve Hot:**
    - **Enjoy:** Serve the yakimeshi hot, directly from the skillet or wok.

Notes:

- **Rice Texture:** Day-old rice works best for fried rice because it's drier and less likely to become mushy. If using freshly cooked rice, let it cool and dry out slightly before using.
- **Vegetable Variations:** Feel free to add other vegetables like bell peppers, corn, mushrooms, or baby corn based on what you have on hand.
- **Meat Alternatives:** You can use any protein you like, such as beef, chicken, pork, shrimp, or tofu. Adjust the cooking time based on the protein you use.
- **Soy Sauce:** Adjust the amount of soy sauce based on your taste preference. You can use low-sodium soy sauce if you're watching your sodium intake.

Yakimeshi is a quick and flavorful dish that's perfect for a weeknight dinner or a lunch. It's customizable, so you can add your favorite ingredients to make it just right for you.

Miso Soup with Clams

Ingredients:

- 4 cups dashi broth (or water with dashi granules)
- 1 cup clams (such as littleneck or Manila clams), scrubbed and rinsed
- 3-4 tablespoons miso paste (white or yellow miso is recommended)
- 1-2 green onions, sliced
- 1/2 cup tofu, cubed (optional)
- 1/2 cup sliced mushrooms (shiitake, enoki, or your choice) (optional)
- Seaweed (wakame), rehydrated and chopped (optional)
- 1 tablespoon soy sauce (optional, for additional seasoning)
- Fresh herbs like parsley or cilantro for garnish (optional)

Instructions:

1. **Prepare the Clams:**
    - **Clean Clams:** Scrub the clams under cold running water to remove any sand or grit. If the clams are not already purged, soak them in a bowl of cold water with a bit of salt for 20-30 minutes to help them expel any sand, then rinse thoroughly.
2. **Make the Broth:**
    - **Heat Dashi:** In a large pot, bring the dashi broth to a gentle simmer over medium heat.
    - **Add Clams:** Add the clams to the pot. Cover and cook until the clams open, about 5-7 minutes. Discard any clams that do not open.
3. **Prepare the Miso:**
    - **Dissolve Miso:** In a small bowl, take a ladleful of the hot broth from the pot and mix it with the miso paste. Stir until the miso is fully dissolved. This helps to incorporate the miso smoothly into the soup without clumps.
4. **Add Miso to Soup:**
    - **Stir in Miso:** Reduce the heat to low and stir the dissolved miso mixture back into the pot. Do not boil the soup after adding the miso, as high heat can destroy the delicate flavors.
5. **Add Optional Ingredients:**
    - **Tofu:** If using tofu, add the cubed tofu to the pot and heat through for a few minutes.
    - **Mushrooms:** If using mushrooms, add them along with the tofu and let them cook until tender.
    - **Seaweed:** If using rehydrated wakame seaweed, add it to the pot and let it heat through for a couple of minutes.
6. **Season and Garnish:**
    - **Taste and Adjust:** Taste the soup and adjust seasoning with a bit of soy sauce if needed. This step is optional, as miso paste is already salty.
    - **Garnish:** Stir in sliced green onions and any other fresh herbs or garnishes you prefer.
7. **Serve:**
    - **Ladle and Enjoy:** Ladle the soup into bowls and serve hot.

Notes:

- **Dashi Broth:** You can use store-bought dashi stock or make your own from kombu (seaweed) and bonito flakes. If using water, you might need to adjust seasoning to make up for the lack of depth that dashi provides.
- **Miso Paste:** White miso (shiro miso) is milder and sweeter, while yellow miso (shinshu miso) is slightly stronger. Choose according to your taste preference.
- **Clam Variations:** Ensure that the clams are fresh and live. Avoid any that have cracked shells or do not open after cooking.
- **Vegetables:** Feel free to add other vegetables like spinach, bok choy, or radishes based on your preference.

Miso Soup with Clams is a wonderful dish that combines the umami-rich miso broth with the subtle, oceanic flavor of clams. It's perfect for a comforting meal and makes for a great addition to any Japanese-inspired menu.

Kake Udon

Ingredients:

For the Broth:

- 4 cups dashi broth (or water with dashi granules)
- 3-4 tablespoons soy sauce
- 2 tablespoons mirin
- 1 tablespoon sake (optional)
- 1 teaspoon sugar (optional)

For the Udon:

- 2 servings of fresh or frozen udon noodles
- 2-3 green onions, sliced
- 1 sheet nori (seaweed), cut into strips (optional)
- 1/2 cup sliced mushrooms (shiitake, enoki, or your choice) (optional)
- Tempura flakes (tenkasu) or pickled ginger for garnish (optional)

Instructions:

1. **Prepare the Broth:**
    - **Heat Dashi:** In a large pot, bring the dashi broth to a gentle simmer over medium heat.
    - **Season Broth:** Add the soy sauce, mirin, and sake to the pot. Stir well. If desired, add a teaspoon of sugar to balance the flavors.
    - **Simmer:** Let the broth simmer for a few minutes to allow the flavors to meld. Adjust seasoning to taste if needed.
2. **Cook the Udon Noodles:**
    - **Prepare Noodles:** If using fresh or frozen udon noodles, cook them according to the package instructions. Fresh noodles typically take 2-3 minutes, while frozen noodles may take a bit longer.
    - **Drain and Rinse:** Once cooked, drain the noodles and rinse under cold water to stop cooking. This helps to remove excess starch.
3. **Assemble the Dish:**
    - **Reheat Broth:** Bring the broth back to a simmer.
    - **Add Noodles:** Add the cooked udon noodles to the simmering broth. Let them heat through for a couple of minutes.
    - **Add Optional Ingredients:** If using mushrooms, add them to the broth and let them cook until tender.
4. **Garnish and Serve:**
    - **Serve:** Divide the udon noodles and broth into serving bowls.

- **Garnish:** Top with sliced green onions, nori strips, tempura flakes, or pickled ginger if desired.
5. **Enjoy:**
    - **Hot and Comforting:** Serve the kake udon hot and enjoy!

Notes:

- **Dashi Broth:** Dashi is a fundamental component of many Japanese dishes. You can use instant dashi granules or make your own from kombu (seaweed) and bonito flakes for a more authentic flavor.
- **Udon Noodles:** Fresh udon noodles are ideal, but frozen or even dried udon can be used if fresh is not available. Adjust cooking times accordingly.
- **Additional Toppings:** Kake udon is versatile, so you can add other toppings like tempura, poached eggs, or leafy greens like spinach or bok choy.
- **Adjusting Flavors:** If you prefer a stronger flavor, increase the soy sauce or add a splash of mirin. If you want a milder taste, reduce the soy sauce and mirin.

Kake Udon is a wonderfully simple dish that showcases the quality of the broth and the texture of the udon noodles. It's perfect for a quick lunch or a comforting dinner, and it can be easily customized with your favorite toppings.

Korean BBQ Beef

Ingredients:

For the Marinade:

- 1/4 cup soy sauce
- 2 tablespoons sugar
- 2 tablespoons honey or corn syrup
- 2 tablespoons sesame oil
- 2 tablespoons rice wine or mirin
- 3 cloves garlic, minced
- 1 tablespoon ginger, minced
- 2 tablespoons gochujang (Korean red chili paste) or Sriracha (optional, for a spicy kick)
- 1/4 cup grated Asian pear or apple (for sweetness and tenderness)
- 1/4 cup chopped green onions
- 1 tablespoon sesame seeds
- 1/2 teaspoon black pepper

For the Beef:

- 1 pound beef sirloin or ribeye, thinly sliced against the grain
- 1 tablespoon vegetable oil (for cooking)
- 1 cup sliced mushrooms (optional)
- 1/2 cup sliced onions
- 1/2 cup sliced bell peppers (optional)

For Serving:

- Steamed rice
- Sliced green onions
- Sesame seeds
- Sliced cucumbers or pickled radishes
- Lettuce leaves for wrapping (optional)

Instructions:

1. **Prepare the Marinade:**
   - **Combine Ingredients:** In a bowl, mix together the soy sauce, sugar, honey, sesame oil, rice wine, minced garlic, minced ginger, gochujang (if using), grated pear or apple, chopped green onions, sesame seeds, and black pepper.
   - **Mix Well:** Stir until the sugar is dissolved and all ingredients are well combined.
2. **Marinate the Beef:**

- **Add Beef to Marinade:** Place the thinly sliced beef into a large resealable plastic bag or a shallow dish.
- **Pour Marinade:** Pour the marinade over the beef, ensuring all slices are coated.
- **Marinate:** Seal the bag or cover the dish and refrigerate for at least 30 minutes, preferably 1-2 hours or overnight for maximum flavor.

3. **Cook the Beef:**
   - **Heat Oil:** Heat a large skillet or grill pan over medium-high heat. Add vegetable oil.
   - **Cook Beef:** Add the marinated beef slices to the skillet in a single layer. If using, add sliced mushrooms, onions, and bell peppers at this stage.
   - **Stir-Fry:** Cook the beef for about 2-3 minutes on each side, or until it's well-browned and cooked through. If using a grill, cook until slightly charred and cooked to your liking.
4. **Serve:**
   - **Prepare Rice:** While the beef is cooking, prepare steamed rice.
   - **Serve Beef:** Serve the cooked Korean BBQ beef over rice, garnished with sliced green onions and sesame seeds.
   - **Add Sides:** Accompany with sliced cucumbers or pickled radishes. Optionally, serve with lettuce leaves for wrapping.

Notes:

- **Beef Cut:** Thinly slicing the beef against the grain ensures tenderness. You can ask your butcher to slice the beef for you, or freeze the beef slightly to make slicing easier.
- **Marinade:** The Asian pear or apple helps tenderize the beef and adds a subtle sweetness. If you can't find an Asian pear, a regular pear or apple will work.
- **Spice Level:** Adjust the amount of gochujang or Sriracha based on your preference for spiciness.
- **Cooking Methods:** If you prefer grilling, preheat your grill and cook the beef over medium-high heat, turning occasionally until cooked through.

Korean BBQ Beef is a delicious and flavorful dish that's perfect for a weeknight dinner or for entertaining. The combination of savory, sweet, and slightly spicy flavors makes it a favorite among many. Enjoy it with a side of rice and your favorite vegetables for a complete meal!

Shiro Ebi (White Shrimp) Tempura

Ingredients:

For the Tempura:

- 8-12 shiro ebi (white shrimp), peeled and deveined (tails intact)
- 1 cup all-purpose flour
- 1/2 cup cornstarch
- 1 large egg, beaten
- 1 cup ice-cold water
- 1/4 teaspoon baking powder
- 1/2 teaspoon salt
- Vegetable oil (for frying)

For the Tempura Batter:

- 1 cup all-purpose flour
- 1/2 cup cornstarch
- 1 large egg, beaten
- 1 cup ice-cold water
- 1/4 teaspoon baking powder
- 1/2 teaspoon salt

For Serving:

- Sea salt or tempura dipping sauce (Tentsuyu)
- Lemon wedges (optional)
- Fresh herbs for garnish (optional)

Instructions:

1. **Prepare the Shrimp:**
   - **Peel and Devein:** Peel the shiro ebi, leaving the tails on for a decorative touch. Devein the shrimp if not already done.
   - **Dry Shrimp:** Pat the shrimp dry with paper towels to remove excess moisture. This helps the batter adhere better.
2. **Prepare the Tempura Batter:**
   - **Mix Dry Ingredients:** In a bowl, whisk together 1 cup all-purpose flour, 1/2 cup cornstarch, baking powder, and salt.
   - **Add Wet Ingredients:** In a separate bowl, lightly beat the egg and then mix it with 1 cup ice-cold water.

- **Combine:** Gently mix the wet ingredients into the dry ingredients until just combined. The batter should be lumpy and not over-mixed. Keep it cold by placing it over a bowl of ice if needed.
3. **Heat the Oil:**
    - **Preheat Oil:** Heat vegetable oil in a deep fryer or a large heavy-bottomed pot to 350°F (175°C). You need enough oil to submerge the shrimp completely.
4. **Batter the Shrimp:**
    - **Coat Shrimp:** Dredge each shrimp lightly in all-purpose flour (this helps the batter adhere) before dipping it into the tempura batter.
    - **Fry Shrimp:** Carefully place the battered shrimp into the hot oil. Fry in batches, being careful not to overcrowd the pot. Fry for about 2-3 minutes, or until golden brown and crispy.
    - **Drain:** Use a slotted spoon to remove the shrimp from the oil and place them on a plate lined with paper towels to drain excess oil.
5. **Serve:**
    - **Garnish:** Sprinkle the tempura shrimp with a pinch of sea salt or serve with tempura dipping sauce (Tentsuyu). Lemon wedges and fresh herbs can be added for extra flavor.
    - **Enjoy:** Serve the shiro ebi tempura immediately while hot and crispy.

Notes:

- **Batter Consistency:** The tempura batter should be lumpy and not too smooth. Over-mixing can lead to a heavy, dense coating.
- **Oil Temperature:** Maintaining the correct oil temperature is crucial for crispy tempura. If the oil is too hot, the batter may burn before the shrimp are cooked; too cold, and the batter will be greasy.
- **Serving Suggestions:** Shiro ebi tempura can be served as an appetizer or as part of a main meal. It pairs well with steamed rice and dipping sauces.

Shiro Ebi Tempura is a sophisticated and delightful dish, perfect for impressing guests or enjoying a special treat. The light, crispy coating complements the sweet, delicate flavor of the white shrimp beautifully.

Saba Misoni (Miso Braised Mackerel)

Ingredients:

- 2 whole mackerel fillets (about 8-10 ounces each), skin on
- 2 tablespoons vegetable oil
- 1/2 cup white miso paste
- 1/4 cup sake (Japanese rice wine)
- 1/4 cup mirin (sweet rice wine)
- 1/4 cup soy sauce
- 2 tablespoons sugar
- 1 cup water
- 2-3 slices of ginger
- 2 green onions, sliced (for garnish)

Instructions:

1. **Prepare the Mackerel:**
   - **Clean Fillets:** Rinse the mackerel fillets under cold water and pat them dry with paper towels. If necessary, cut the fillets into portions for easier handling.
2. **Make the Miso Sauce:**
   - **Combine Ingredients:** In a bowl, mix together the white miso paste, sake, mirin, soy sauce, sugar, and water until the miso and sugar are fully dissolved.
3. **Cook the Mackerel:**
   - **Heat Oil:** In a large skillet or braising pan, heat the vegetable oil over medium heat.
   - **Sear Fish:** Add the mackerel fillets, skin-side down, and sear until the skin is crispy and browned, about 3-4 minutes. Flip the fillets and cook for another 1-2 minutes. Remove the fillets from the pan and set aside.
4. **Prepare the Braising Liquid:**
   - **Add Miso Sauce:** In the same skillet or braising pan, add the miso sauce mixture. Stir to combine with any browned bits left in the pan.
   - **Add Ginger:** Add the slices of ginger to the sauce.
5. **Braise the Mackerel:**
   - **Return Fish to Pan:** Place the seared mackerel fillets back into the pan, skin-side up.
   - **Simmer:** Bring the sauce to a gentle simmer. Reduce the heat to low, cover, and cook for about 15-20 minutes, or until the mackerel is cooked through and tender. The sauce should thicken slightly.
6. **Serve:**
   - **Garnish:** Transfer the mackerel fillets to serving plates. Spoon the braising sauce over the top and garnish with sliced green onions.
   - **Accompany:** Serve with steamed rice and your favorite vegetable side dishes.

Notes:

- **Miso Type:** White miso (shiro miso) is preferred for its milder and sweeter flavor, but you can use other types of miso if you prefer a stronger taste.
- **Mackerel Alternatives:** If mackerel is not available, you can substitute with other fatty fish like salmon or trout, adjusting the cooking time as needed.
- **Adjusting Sweetness:** If you prefer a sweeter sauce, you can add a bit more sugar or mirin. For a saltier flavor, increase the soy sauce slightly.
- **Leftovers:** Saba misoni makes great leftovers. The flavors continue to develop as it sits, so it's excellent for meal prepping or enjoying the next day.

Saba Misoni is a comforting and savory dish that's perfect for a home-cooked Japanese meal. The combination of tender mackerel and flavorful miso sauce creates a deliciously satisfying experience.

Nasu Dengaku (Miso Grilled Eggplant)

Ingredients:

- 2 large eggplants
- 3 tablespoons miso paste (white or red miso)
- 2 tablespoons mirin (sweet rice wine)
- 1 tablespoon sake (Japanese rice wine) or water
- 1 tablespoon sugar
- 1 tablespoon sesame oil
- 1 tablespoon vegetable oil
- 2 tablespoons sesame seeds (for garnish)
- 2 green onions, sliced (for garnish)
- Pickled ginger or shiso leaves (optional, for garnish)

Instructions:

1. **Prepare the Eggplant:**
    - **Slice Eggplant:** Cut the eggplants in half lengthwise. If the eggplants are very large, you can cut them into quarters.
    - **Score:** Lightly score the flesh of the eggplants in a crosshatch pattern to allow the miso glaze to penetrate better.
2. **Make the Miso Glaze:**
    - **Combine Ingredients:** In a small saucepan, combine the miso paste, mirin, sake (or water), sugar, and sesame oil.
    - **Heat:** Cook over medium heat, stirring frequently, until the mixture is well combined and slightly thickened. This should take about 3-4 minutes. Remove from heat and let cool.
3. **Prepare the Eggplant:**
    - **Brush with Oil:** Brush the cut sides of the eggplant with vegetable oil to prevent sticking and ensure even grilling or broiling.
4. **Grill or Broil the Eggplant:**
    - **Preheat:** Preheat your grill to medium heat or your broiler to high.
    - **Grill or Broil:** Place the eggplant halves cut-side down on the grill or under the broiler. Grill or broil for about 4-5 minutes, or until the cut side is nicely charred and the eggplant is beginning to soften.
    - **Flip:** Turn the eggplants cut-side up. Brush generously with the miso glaze.
5. **Finish Cooking:**
    - **Grill or Broil Again:** Continue grilling or broiling for another 4-5 minutes, or until the eggplant is tender and the miso glaze is caramelized and bubbling. Keep an eye on it to prevent burning.
6. **Serve:**

- **Garnish:** Transfer the grilled eggplants to a serving plate. Sprinkle with sesame seeds and sliced green onions. Garnish with pickled ginger or shiso leaves if desired.
- **Enjoy:** Serve warm as an appetizer, side dish, or part of a larger Japanese meal.

Notes:

- **Miso Type:** White miso (shiro miso) is milder and sweeter, while red miso (aka miso) is stronger and saltier. Choose according to your flavor preference.
- **Eggplant Preparation:** Salting the eggplant before cooking can help reduce bitterness and improve texture, but this step is optional. If you choose to salt, let the eggplant sit for 30 minutes, then rinse and pat dry before proceeding.
- **Broiling vs. Grilling:** Both methods work well. Grilling imparts a smoky flavor, while broiling gives a more direct caramelization.
- **Adjusting Sweetness:** If you prefer a sweeter glaze, adjust the amount of sugar or mirin to taste.

Nasu Dengaku is a delightful way to enjoy eggplant with its rich miso glaze. This dish pairs well with steamed rice and is a great addition to any Japanese-inspired meal.

Wasabi Mashed Potatoes

Ingredients:

- 2 pounds (900 grams) potatoes (Yukon Gold or Russet are good choices)
- 1/2 cup (120 ml) milk (whole or 2% for creaminess)
- 1/4 cup (60 grams) unsalted butter
- 1-2 tablespoons wasabi paste (adjust to taste)
- Salt and black pepper to taste
- 2 tablespoons chopped chives (optional, for garnish)

Instructions:

1. **Prepare the Potatoes:**
   - **Peel and Cut:** Peel the potatoes and cut them into roughly equal-sized chunks (about 1-inch pieces).
   - **Cook Potatoes:** Place the potatoes in a large pot and cover with cold water. Add a pinch of salt.
   - **Boil:** Bring to a boil over high heat. Reduce the heat to a simmer and cook for about 15-20 minutes, or until the potatoes are tender and can be easily pierced with a fork.
2. **Drain and Mash:**
   - **Drain Potatoes:** Drain the cooked potatoes in a colander and let them sit for a minute or two to allow excess moisture to evaporate.
   - **Mash Potatoes:** Return the potatoes to the pot or place them in a large mixing bowl. Mash the potatoes with a potato masher until smooth. For a creamier texture, you can use a potato ricer or food mill.
3. **Prepare the Wasabi Mixture:**
   - **Heat Milk and Butter:** In a small saucepan, heat the milk and butter over medium heat until the butter is melted and the mixture is warm.
   - **Mix Wasabi:** Stir in the wasabi paste into the milk and butter mixture. Start with 1 tablespoon of wasabi paste and taste, adding more if you want additional heat.
4. **Combine and Season:**
   - **Mix Together:** Gradually add the warm milk and butter mixture to the mashed potatoes, stirring continuously until the desired consistency is reached.
   - **Season:** Season with salt and black pepper to taste. Adjust the wasabi according to your heat preference.
5. **Serve:**
   - **Garnish:** Transfer the wasabi mashed potatoes to a serving dish. Garnish with chopped chives if desired.
   - **Enjoy:** Serve warm as a side dish with your favorite main course.

Notes:

- **Wasabi Paste:** The amount of wasabi paste can be adjusted based on your preference for spiciness. Start with a smaller amount and gradually increase as needed.
- **Potato Texture:** For extra creamy mashed potatoes, you can add a bit more milk or butter. If you prefer a chunkier texture, mash less thoroughly.
- **Substitute for Wasabi Paste:** If you don't have wasabi paste, you can use prepared horseradish as an alternative, though it will have a slightly different flavor profile.
- **Make Ahead:** These mashed potatoes can be made ahead of time and reheated gently. If needed, add a splash of milk to loosen them up before serving.

Wasabi Mashed Potatoes offer a unique and spicy twist on a classic side dish, making them a great addition to any meal where you want to add a bit of excitement. They pair wonderfully with grilled meats, seafood, or even as a bold side for a vegetarian main course.

Shiso and Almond Cookies

Ingredients:

- 1 cup (120 grams) all-purpose flour
- 1/2 cup (60 grams) almond meal or finely ground almonds
- 1/2 cup (115 grams) unsalted butter, softened
- 1/2 cup (100 grams) granulated sugar
- 1/4 cup (50 grams) brown sugar
- 1 large egg
- 1 teaspoon vanilla extract
- 1/2 teaspoon baking powder
- 1/4 teaspoon salt
- 1/4 cup (20 grams) chopped almonds (for topping)
- 1/4 cup (15 grams) finely chopped fresh shiso leaves (about 10-12 leaves)

Instructions:

1. **Preheat Oven:**
   - **Heat Oven:** Preheat your oven to 350°F (175°C). Line a baking sheet with parchment paper or a silicone baking mat.
2. **Prepare the Dough:**
   - **Cream Butter and Sugars:** In a large mixing bowl, cream together the softened butter, granulated sugar, and brown sugar until light and fluffy.
   - **Add Egg and Vanilla:** Beat in the egg and vanilla extract until well combined.
   - **Mix Dry Ingredients:** In a separate bowl, whisk together the flour, almond meal, baking powder, and salt.
   - **Combine:** Gradually add the dry ingredients to the wet ingredients, mixing until just combined.
   - **Add Shiso and Almonds:** Fold in the chopped shiso leaves until evenly distributed. If desired, you can also fold in a small portion of chopped almonds into the dough for extra crunch.
3. **Shape the Cookies:**
   - **Form Cookies:** Using a tablespoon or a cookie scoop, drop rounded balls of dough onto the prepared baking sheet, spacing them about 2 inches apart.
   - **Flatten Slightly:** Flatten each cookie slightly with the back of a spoon or your fingers to form discs.
   - **Top with Almonds:** Sprinkle the tops of the cookies with the remaining chopped almonds for added texture and visual appeal.
4. **Bake:**
   - **Bake Cookies:** Bake in the preheated oven for 10-12 minutes, or until the edges are golden brown and the centers are set.

- **Cool:** Allow the cookies to cool on the baking sheet for a few minutes before transferring them to a wire rack to cool completely.
5. **Serve:**
    - **Enjoy:** Serve the Shiso and Almond Cookies as a unique and flavorful treat with tea or coffee.

Notes:

- **Shiso Leaves:** Shiso leaves have a distinctive flavor that can be somewhat similar to basil or mint. If fresh shiso leaves are unavailable, you can use dried shiso or omit it entirely, though the flavor will differ.
- **Almond Meal:** Almond meal adds a nutty richness to the cookies. If you prefer a more pronounced almond flavor, you can increase the amount of almond meal or add a bit of almond extract.
- **Cookie Texture:** If the dough seems too soft, refrigerate it for about 30 minutes before baking to help the cookies hold their shape.

Shiso and Almond Cookies offer a creative and aromatic twist on traditional cookies. The combination of shiso's unique flavor and the crunch of almonds makes them a delightful and memorable treat.

www.ingramcontent.com/pod-product-compliance
Lightning Source LLC
LaVergne TN
LVHW081557060526
838201LV00054B/1929